Praise for Blake Hayes

Blake Hayes has used his God-given ability of thinking, writing, and reasoning to produce an excellent in-depth study of the pre-exilic prophets. His research is thorough, and his ability to tie the strengths and foibles of these ancients to our current culture is commendable. Whether you are a devoted Bible history buff or not, you will enjoy and appreciate this book!

> — Steve Lusk, Discipleship Minister, Red
> Bank Church of Christ, Chattanooga,
> Tennessee

The highlight of the book is the opening chapter, which is a very helpful summary of the world and work of the Old Testament prophets. The prophetic messages can be very challenging to decipher without the proper larger context. Blake has done some of the heavy lifting to aid in our understanding of the details and the application of their timeless lessons to modern believers. This is a perfect complement in Bible classes and for individual study. May God bless you as you read and study His Word and great books like this one that assist in your learning!

> — Tommy Stone, Preaching Minister, Red
> Bank Church of Christ, Chattanooga,
> Tennessee

The Pre-Exilic Prophets

A Homiletical Commentary

Blake Hayes

CYPRESS
PUBLICATIONS
An Imprint of Heritage Christian University Press

Copyright © 2026 by Blake Hayes

Cataloging-in-Publication Data

Hayes, Blake

The Pre-Exilic Prophets: a homiletical commentary / Blake Hayes.

p. cm.

ISBN: 979-8-89733-021-8 (pbk.); 979-8-89733-022-5 (ebook)

1. Bible. Prophets—Commentaries. I. Author. II. Title.

224.07—dc20

Cover design by Nora Stone.

Kayla Campbell sketched the map seen in the opening pages.

Cypress Publications
3625 Helton Drive
PO Box HCU
Florence, AL 35630

www.hcu.edu

To Mady, Mila, and Sophia.
Hosea 6:3

Acknowledgments

This book would not have been possible without the support and encouragement of so many friends, family, and teachers. I thank Dr. Justin Rogers for his encouragement to get this book written and for suggesting it be published. Being able to learn from him in several different settings has been a blessing for both my academic journey and my personal faith. Dr. Kirk Brothers also deserves special mention for his impact on me and so many other men and women of faith. Without his help, this book would not have been possible.

I am thankful to Steve Lusk and Tommy Stone for reading the earliest versions of the book and making helpful comments. Laurie Newby, Whitney Tompkins, and Amy Hayes all read through the final draft and provided extremely helpful feedback and encouragement throughout the process. The Thursday morning Bible study group at Red Bank church of Christ listened with patience and thoughtfulness to the lecture form of the material and made valuable comments throughout the class. The press committee at Heritage Christian kindly guided me along this unfamiliar process. This project would not be available without their effort and backing.

Nora Stone and Kayla Campbell deserve special praise for their artwork on the project. Nora created a beautiful and meaningful cover art for the book, and Kayla generously sketched the map seen in the opening pages.

Finally, and most importantly, I am thankful for my wife, Mady, for her unending love and support.

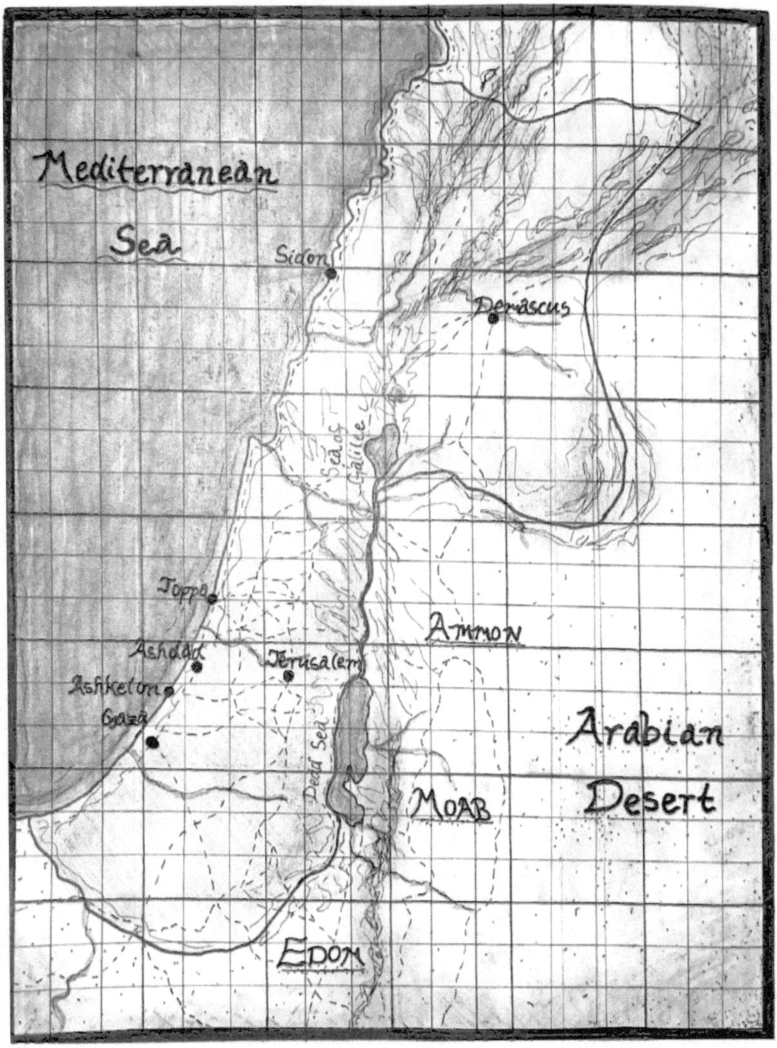

Mediterranean
Sea
Sidon
Damascus
Sea of Galilee
Joppa
Ashdod
Jerusalem
Ashkelon
Gaza
Dead Sea
Ammon
Arabian
Desert
Moab
Edom

Introduction

There have been several attempts in the study of the prophets to try and narrow their task and mission. Some want to describe these men as social critics, calling out the sins of society. Some see them as seers, bringing their vision of the future into the present. Some describe them as a mouthpiece, simply relaying a message from God. The list could go on—preacher, economic critic, intercessor—and each of these is true, but to reduce the life of the prophets to a single one of these categories misunderstands the richness and depth of their calling. Each prophet is unique—not only in the way he speaks and writes, but also in the life he lives and the particular path his ministry takes. Despite the large amount of diversity in the lives and messages of the prophets, there is also a deep unity found throughout this section of scripture. Each prophet seeks to turn the rebellious, calloused hearts of the people of Israel and Judah back to their God. Tragically, they are unified in their failure to complete this task. The persistent rebellion on behalf of the people ultimately leads them into exile. Soon, foreign nations will invade their cities and carry the people out of the very land God had given them. Like the beginning of Exodus, God's people once again find themselves in an unfamiliar land, waiting for deliverance.

This book will focus on the pre-exilic prophets—those who came to warn the nation before the exile took place. We will move (as accurately as possible) chronologically through these prophetic books, following the nation along the painful path toward exile. Along the way, you may notice the prophetic message growing increasingly sorrowful and mournful as these men witness corruption take hold of the nation. But all is not dark—light and hope gently linger beneath the surface, waiting to break through. As Christians, we can read these pages of grief and know that this is not the final word. God will come again for His people.

Not only are these prophets unique in their message, but they also appear at different times throughout the history of Israel and Judah. A basic understanding of the historical background of each book can help unlock deeper layers of meaning in the words of the prophets. To aid in this, several sections throughout the commentary will pause to focus specifically on the historical setting of the book. These are simply meant to offer moments for deeper exploration, but are by no means necessary to understanding the chapter as a whole. This commentary is also not meant to take the place of the actual books they summarize. This book is best used as a companion to help guide you as you read through the prophets themselves. This is also not a book to simply dispense information. The words of the prophets are meant to pierce the heart. Their words are not simply there to be read, but to elicit reflection by the reader. Questions are included at the end of each section for personal or group use to help digest the message and reflect on our own lives. May we approach each book with humble hearts as we seek to learn from these courageous men who were chosen and sent by God to turn the hearts of His people.

Contents

Chapter 1

The World of the Prophets

The prophet is a person, not a microphone. He is endowed with a mission, with the power of a word not his own that accounts for his greatness—but also with temperament, concern, character, and individuality. As there was no resisting the impact of divine inspiration, so at times, there was no resisting the vortex of his own temperament. The word of God reverberated in the voice of man. The prophet's task is to convey a divine view, but as a person, he is a point of view. He speaks from the perspective of God as perceived from the perspective of his own situation. We must seek to understand ... not only what he said but also what he lived.[1]

— Abraham Heschel, *The Prophets*

---

1. Abraham Heschel, *The Prophets* (New York: HarperCollins, 2001), Kindle edition, xxii.

THE BIBLICAL PROPHETS contain some of the most beautiful and impactful verses in all of scripture, but they can also be some of the most difficult books of the Bible to read and understand. Bouncing back and forth between their current climate and the world to come, a masterful use of Hebrew poetry, the employment of creative imagery, and many other elements fill the pages with color but also demand that we not settle for a superficial reading. One of the most crucial and challenging pieces to understanding the prophets is to have a solid understanding of the world around the prophets. These men do not appear in a vacuum but are a product and response to the social, moral, and political corruption within Israel and Judah.

Understanding the world in which the prophets spoke will help us, as readers, better comprehend the message that is brought before God's people. There are three nations that have a significant impact on the divided kingdom of Israel during the time of the prophets: Assyria, Babylon, and Egypt. Our attention will focus on Assyria and Babylon since these are the dominant powers at the time, and will be the two nations that take God's people into exile. Each of these three nations would provide a test for God's people. Who has their trust? Whom do they fear? Where is their hope? The words and actions of the prophets will slowly reveal the answer to these key questions over time.

The Divided Kingdom of Israel and Judah

The greatest threats to a nation are often internal rather than external. This is proven painfully true for the nation of Israel in the years following King David's reign. After the division of the kingdom following Solomon's death (Israel to the North/Judah to the South), these two nations would remain separate with two significant differences: Israel had nine different dynasties (ruling families) while Judah only had one (the Davidic line), and Israel set up opposing ways/places of worship while Judah maintains temple worship.[2] These differences will play a huge role in the life of each nation. "The presence of the Davidic covenant in Judah and its absence in the north explains why the kingship in the north is plagued with instability and violence in contrast to the south."[3] When reading through the historical books in the Old Testament, notice how all the kings of Judah are compared or contrasted with David, while the northern kings are not, showing the importance of keeping the royal lineage. Even with these facts, it is important not to romanticize the kingdom of Judah in comparison to Israel's evil. Judah, too, is visited by prophets who deliver a message of warning and repentance, not praise.

Though the entire kingdom was given to Rehoboam following Solomon's death, a series of bad decisions and growing tensions led Jeroboam to lead a rebellion against the new king. 1 Kings 12 records the story, which ends with Rehoboam keeping control of Judah and Jeroboam as the new king of Israel. Neither ruler garners a favorable image when their stories are told, but it is Jeroboam who will eventually become the stereotypical image of evil for following kings in Judah. His reign is characterized by five evil acts that set his actions apart: he established alternate sites of worship at Dan and Bethel, built other shrines at high places, appointed non-Levitical priests, instituted a new feast "like the festival in Judah," and offered sacrifices on the altars he built (1 Kings 12:25–33). Each of these actions served to divide the northern

---

2. This is not to say that Judah resists idols. They also fall victim to the sin and influence of idol worship, but the distinguishing factor is that they also have the temple and maintain temple worship—Israel does not.

3. Bruce Waltke, *An Old Testament Theology: An Exegetical, Canonical, and Thematic Approach* (Grand Rapids: Zondervan Academic, 2007), 752.

kingdom even further from their brother to the south. Rehoboam begins his reign on a similar path but is humbled by the invasion of Shishak (an Egyptian king—2 Chronicles 12:12) and repents. His reign will become a common refrain for the kings and people of Judah who edge on corruption but turn at the last second in an effort to repent. That cycle, as you would expect, was doomed to fail and would eventually lead to the destruction and exile of Judah.

The two prominent dynasties of the northern kingdom are the Omride and Jehu dynasties. The Omride dynasty lasted from King Omri (885–874 BCE) to Joram (852–841 BCE) and was a time of great evil and corruption. Omri, upon his ascension to the throne, brings some stability to a nation that has exhausted itself through conflict with Judah. He establishes Samaria as the capital city and marries his son Ahab to Jezebel, the daughter of the king of Tyre. This move would allow pagan worship to truly take hold in Israel as Jezebel sets up a temple to Baal in Samaria and seeks to eradicate the worship of Israel's God.

King Jehu (841–814 BCE) brought a bloody end to the Omri family but failed to rid the nation of the Baal worship they established. The highlight of the Jehu dynasty is the reign of King Jeroboam II (782–753 BCE), who is regarded by many historians to be the most capable king in Israel's history.[4] He successfully brought economic and military success to Israel, but was spiritually deficient and would begin the rapid downfall of the northern kingdom. In the final ten years following Jeroboam II's death, Israel would see five different kings sit on the throne, with three of those kings seizing it through violence.

---

4. Leon J. Wood, *A Survey of Israel's History*, rev. ed. (Grand Rapids: Zondervan, 1986), 276.

Israel's capital city, Samaria, would eventually fall to Assyria, with the inhabitants being taken into exile in 722 BCE.

The southern kingdom of Judah receives the most attention in the prophets around the time of Ahaz and his descendants. King Ahaz rises to power at the dawn of Assyrian domination. In the heat of key political and military moves, Ahaz turns his back on Israel and other nations attempting to form an anti-Assyrian coalition and bends the knee to Tiglath-Pileser III of Assyria. This move would mean allegiance to Assyria and the expectation of heavy tribute paid to the foreign king. Ahaz not only makes unwise political moves but also proves to be a dark spot in the line of Judah's kings. He succumbs to worshiping idols and later robs the temple to send tribute to Assyria (2 Kings 16:2–18). His son, Hezekiah, reverses the political and spiritual downfalls of his father, and with the rise of a new Assyrian king, he attempts to rebel against the dominating world power. His efforts of rebellion prove futile, but due to his defensive strategy (reinforcing the city walls and the construction of Hezekiah's tunnel) and divine intervention, he is able to hold off an Assyrian invasion.

Hezekiah's son, Manasseh, continues the cycle and reverses all his father had done before him. Manasseh is remembered as the most corrupt king in Judah's history, who filled the city walls with innocent blood (2 Kings 21:16). He left such a dark imprint on Judah's history that 2 Kings 24:1–3 contributes the exile specifically to Manasseh's sins. The cycle of good and bad kings continues with Josiah as he begins a spiritual reformation within the city while also bringing political stability to the nation. However, the period following Josiah's reign is chaotic both for Judah and the world stage at large. A monumental event, the fall of Assyria (612 BCE), led to a fight for power with Babylon emerging as the next Goliath in world history. They would eventually march on Judah and capture the capital city of Jerusalem in 586 BCE. This would begin a stretch in Israel's history known as the exilic period, where God's people lived as exiles in Babylon until they were released by King Cyrus of Persia in 539 BCE.

The Assyrian Empire

The Assyrians, like all other nations spread throughout the Ancient Near East, have a fascinating and lengthy history documenting their rise to power. Scholars have divided that history into 3 eras separated by key events that shape the nation. The climax of that story is known as the Neo-Assyrian Period, and this is the part of Assyrian history that has the most influence on the Biblical story, especially the prophets. This period is a witness to 19 different Assyrian kings, but only five of those played a significant role in the prophets.

The first king was Shalmaneser III, who reigned from 859–824 BCE. His title comes not because he is a descendant of the Shalmaneser family, but because Assyrian kings began the practice of assuming the names of ancient kings of the "Old Assyrian Period" when they rose to the throne.[5] His famous Black Obelisk mentions his military successes over Ahab of Israel and several other surrounding city-states. His campaigns into the west probably stretched his borders too far and would prove difficult for subsequent kings to manage. After a lengthy lull in power and influence, Assyria would come back even stronger under the leadership of Tiglath-Pileser III (745–727 BCE). He would prove to be the most dominant king in Assyrian history. During his rule, he quelled surrounding

---

5.   Bill Arnold and Brent Strawn, eds., *The World Around the Old Testament: The People and Places of the Ancient Near East* (Grand Rapids: Baker Academic, 2016), 41.

revolts that began during the period of weakness after Shalmaneser III formally took the Babylonian throne, and defeated an anti-Assyrian coalition led in part by King Pekah of Israel. Following him, both Shalmaneser V (727–722 BCE) and Sargon II (722–705 BCE) would take advantage of a weakened Israel nation and take the northern kingdom into exile in 722 BCE following the destruction of Samaria.

The final king deserving our attention is Sennacherib (705–681). Reigning after the fall of Samaria (722 BCE), Sennacherib made his largest impact through his attacks against Judah. After the fall of his father before him (Sargon II), Judah took a chance to rebel against the overbearing nation. The attempt proved terribly unsuccessful and brought about Assyria's devastating western campaign into Judah territory. Sennacherib began his march toward Jerusalem with the intent to plunder the city, destroying every town and village along his way. Through divine intervention, the city of Jerusalem was spared, and Sennacherib returned home, where he was eventually murdered by his brothers (Isaiah 36–39; 2 Kings 18:13–20:19). Though spared from defeat, Judah would become an Assyrian vassal state, which required them to pay heavier tribute to Assyria. This tribute often came in the form of heavy taxation upon the people.

> Generally, the goal of the Assyrian Empire was not merely to maximize its territory, but to extract as much wealth as possible from outlying areas .... It worked very much like a mafia protection racket: kings of smaller nations had to pay the tribute or be deposed, and likely killed."[6]

---

6. Arnold and Strawn, *World*, 41. This would characterize the reigns of Pekah and Hosea in Israel.

The Babylonian Empire

The Babylonians were a consistent thorn in the side of the Assyrians throughout the duration of their reign. After years of war and oppression, Babylon would eventually become the nation to gain control following the downfall of the mighty Assyrians. Like Assyria, Babylon also has a long history that reaches a climax in the Neo-Babylonian period. During the reign of Hezekiah in Judah, Babylon began a slow rise to power, perhaps even seeking to strike an alliance with Judah against Assyria (2 Kings 20:12; Isaiah 39). It wouldn't be until the reign of Josiah that Babylon would march onto the world stage under the reign of Nabopolassar (625–605). His crowning achievement would be the overthrow of Assyria's capital, Nineveh, and with that the downfall of the nation (612 BCE). Following the conquest, Babylon turned their focus inward, choosing to reinforce internal stability rather than extending her territory.

It would be Nabopolassar's son, Nebuchadnezzar II, who would step into a more imperialistic mindset. He would essentially take over the entirety of the Assyrian empire by defeating Egypt—the main rival for power—in the battle of Carchemish (605 BCE). From this date to the fall of Jerusalem in 586 BCE, Judah would be taken in four separate waves as exiles to Babylon. This was a continuation of the Assyrian practice to deport mass sections of the population and integrate them into Babylonian society; a practice that was ended with King Cyrus of Persia, who would then allow the deported people of Israel and Judah to return home and even rebuild the temple. Babylon has the most significant impact on the exilic prophets like Ezekiel and Daniel.

What Manner of Man Is the Prophet?

Amid these extremely turbulent times, the biblical prophets make their abrupt appearance. It is important to remember that the political stage of their day is anything but static. Rather, constantly changing powers and revolts would leave many questioning whom they should trust for guidance and protection. Should we lean on the mighty Assyrian nation, even though they are known for their brutal treatment of foreigners and heavy taxes? Should we trust in the rising Babylonian revolts to provide a reprieve from Assyrian domination? Or should we rally with those around us to establish our own power? It is in these times that the prophets not only urge God's people to repent but also to put their hope and trust in the God of their fathers to deliver and protect them.

To better understand the prophet's message, it is beneficial to not only understand their history but also to look at who the prophets are as individuals. This section adopts heavily from the work of Abraham Heschel and his book *The Prophets,* where he examines "What manner of man is the prophet?"[7] In that section, he draws several contrasts between the prophets and their audience (both ancient and modern) to show how their message, lives, and hearts differed from those around them. Not only do these contrasts help us understand the prophets, but they also reinforce why the prophetic message is still valuable in our world today.

1. The people are *lenient* toward sin, while the prophets are *intolerant* of the slightest injustice. We tend to champion civility over confrontation, but the prophets don't hold back in their evaluation

---

7. Heschel, *Prophets,* 3–31.

of the people. One of the initial reactions to the words of the prophets is to be taken aback by their harshness. To the prophet, even the smallest of offenses becomes a plank in the eyes of the people that must be removed. It is tempting to view the prophetic message as pedantic and abrasive, but as Heschel says, "If such deep sensitivity to evil is to be called hysterical, what name should be given to the abysmal indifference to evil which the prophet bewails?"[8] Complacency is deadly; urgency becomes the prophetic response.

2. We tend to view God as *stoic*, while the prophets paint God as *exploding with emotion*. The God of our imagination can often be monotonous (even in a positive light), but in the prophets, you see a passionate God who moves between deep agony and overwhelming love for His people. "Man is rebellious and full of iniquity, and yet so cherished is he that God, the Creator of heaven and earth, is saddened when forsaken by him. Profound and intimate is God's love for man, and yet harsh and dreadful can be His wrath."[9]

3. We view our fate as *divorced* from those around us, while the prophets know their fate to be *united* with their people. "This is the secret of the prophet's style: his life and soul are at stake in what he says and in what is going to happen to what he says."[10] The prophet truly goes down with his ship. There is passion in his words because these are his

---

8. Heschel, *Prophets*, 5.
9. Heschel, *Prophets*, 5.
10. Heschel, *Prophets*, 7.

people. There is lament because, for some, this too will be their exile. It is true that the prophets live in a far more communal world than our own, but how would our relationships change if we helped bear one another's burdens rather than dismissing them as someone else's problem?

4. For us, repetition is *monotonous*. For the prophets, repetition is a *plea* for repentance and revival. Reading the prophets can feel like you are hearing the same message over and over again, and oftentimes, you are. However, the message is increasingly sorrowful with each repetition, reminding us of how the prophetic message fell upon the deaf ears of a calloused people. Though the prophets urgently reiterate their message, the people walk further and further away.

5. To us, the glory of a nation lies in its *wealth and power*. To the prophets, the glory of a nation lies in the *knowledge of God*. "Let not the wise man glory in his wisdom, let not the mighty man glory in his might, let not the rich man glory in his riches; but let him who glories, glory in this, that he understands and knows Me, that I am the LORD who practices kindness, justice, and righteousness in the earth; for in these things I delight, says the LORD" (Jeremiah 9:23–24). A nation will not truly be God's people without a deep and true knowledge of Him. Though a nation, people, or church do many things in God's name, without a true relationship with the Creator, the answer is the same: "Depart from me, I never knew you" (Matthew 7:23).

6. We tend to view the prophets as *fortune-tellers*,
   while the prophets see themselves as *forth-tellers*.
   Though the prophets occasionally tell of future
   events, the "prominent theme is exhortation, not
   mere prediction."[11] The prophet's primary role is to
   bring God's message to His people so they might
   repent. They will often employ predictions and
   signs of things to come, but only to bear witness to
   the truth of their message for the present.

7. Modern thought tends to *extenuate* personal
   responsibility, while the prophets emphasize that
   few are guilty, but *all are responsible*. The prophets
   see moral corruption within the community as a
   breakdown in our responsibility toward one
   another. How does that message apply in our
   churches? In our families? In our personal
   relationships?

8. To us, God's presence is a moment of *peace and
   bliss*. To the prophets, God's presence is both
   fearful and challenging. "The prophet disdains
   those for whom God's presence is comfort and
   security; to him it is a challenge, an incessant
   demand. God is compassion, not compromise;
   justice, though not inclemency." [12] The presence of
   God with His people was a gift that was taken for
   granted over time. The prophets insisted that God's
   presence was part of a covenant that must be kept.
   God's presence, while a wonderful and joyful
   reality, is also a challenge to live as He desires and
   walk in His footsteps.

---

11. Heschel, *Prophets*, 14.
12. Heschel, *Prophets*, 19.

9. It is easy for us to view God as *distant* and far off. Through the prophets, the God of Israel is *revealed*. The words and message of the prophets give a window into the character of God that no other work had or would accomplish until the arrival of Christ. "This is the marvel of the prophet's work: in his words the invisible God becomes audible."[13]

10. Finally, we view worship as *primary*, while the prophets view worship as *secondary*. "The external liturgy is of no avail apart from the internal."[14] The prophets make the bold claim that all elements of worship are useless if not preceded and combined with love for one another. Worship is not a cover-up for sin, but a response from the heart of God's people.

---

13. Heschel, *Prophets*, 26.
14. Waltke, *Theology*, 815.

Chapter 2

The Book of Jonah

The whale steals it. We forget the allegorical point of the story (Babylon engulfing disobedient Israel), we don't much care about whether or not Nineveh was saved, or what happened to the regurgitated penitent; but we remember the whale.[1]

— Julian Barnes, *A History of the World in*
10 1/2 Chapters

WHAT COMES to mind when you hear the name "Jonah the prophet"? Though the large fish often dominates our retelling of the story, it often looms larger in our memory than it does in the narrative itself, taking up only three verses in the entire story. It's not wrong for our minds to go there so quickly, but it is a misstep if we stop at the fish and go no further. The common temptation with much of the Old Testament (especially the narrative sections) is to skim the surface of the text

---

1. Julian Barnes, *A History of the World in* 10 ½ *Chapters* (New York: Random House, 1990), 177.

and neglect a slow, reflective reading of the story. And while our reflection often produces more questions than it does answers, it also forces us to see parts of ourselves within the story and within the characters we are often quick to judge. Jonah is no exception.

This odd story of a wayward prophet leaves the reader with many unanswered questions (the book even ends on an unanswered question), but the irony of the narrative causes us to examine and re-examine ourselves, asking: Are we as disobedient as the prophet? Are we as faithful as the pagans? Are we as penitent as the wicked city? Who truly deserves God's grace and mercy? Immediately, we can see that the story is much deeper than the trials between a fish and a prophet. While the book is unique in many ways, it will serve as the perfect beginning to the dense prophetic era of 8th-century Israel and Judah, as the readers are forced to grapple with the difficult questions it presents.

Jonah comes into the story during the reign of Jeroboam II. This was a time of great peace and financial prosperity in Israel. Not by coincidence, this was also a time of weakness for the soon-to-be-dominant nation of Assyria. It is at this point that the God of Israel comes to Jonah, son of Amittai (meaning, "dove, son of faithfulness"), and commissions him to prophecy. However, he would not go to his own people, but to his bitter enemy to the northeast, Nineveh, a major city in the nation of Assyria. From here on, irony floods the book as we are forced to expect the unexpected.

* * *

Assyria and the Assyrians

Nineveh became the capital of Assyria at the height of its empire in the 7th Century BCE in the years following Jonah's ministry. It was the largest city in the Near East up to that point until it was eventually dethroned by Babylon. Two words describe the nation of Assyria at this time: brutal and domineering. To them, the greatest tool for maintaining control was fear. They adorned their city gates, palaces, and temples with intimidating reliefs depicting their brutality in battle and the merciless torture of those who survived. Those subject to Assyrian rule "were made to gaze on these monuments either as erected in their own lands or as arranged in procession on the walls of the palace complexes at Nineveh."[2]

Bent on extending territory and gaining wealth, Shalmaneser III (r. 858–842) of Assyria led a campaign against the West, but the local kings rallied together and led a revolt and blocked his attempts. Included in this rebellion was King Ahab of Israel. Going off Shalmaneser's own records (which probably paint him in a better light than reality), he eventually gained victory over the coalition and the Black Obelisk of Shalmaneser III records him taking tribute from Jehu of Israel, who reigned in the years following Ahab. Assyria was probably not quite strong enough to handle this expansion and battle, so years of instability followed. "Not coincidentally, this period of Assyrian disarray and attention to the north coincides with the long and apparently successful reign of Jeroboam II in Israel (r. 788–748)."[3] This serves as the setting for the book of Jonah.

---

2. Arnold and Strawn, *World*, 39.
3. Arnold and Strawn, *World*, 47.

* * *

The book opens with the formulaic phrase, "And the word of the LORD came ..." that is often found throughout the prophets, marking their divine call. What usually serves to ignite the prophetic task proves to be Jonah's greatest burden. After receiving his call, he immediately flees to Joppa and boards a ship toward Tarshish (perhaps located in modern-day Spain), as far west as possible, in order to flee "from the presence of the LORD" as the narrative painstakingly reminds us. The repetition of the phrase could indicate his determination to get away or even his belief that an escape from God was actually possible (In Jonah's day, many believed that the gods were bound by the borders of their nation, so fleeing Judah meant fleeing God). He pays the fare and goes "down into the ship," which begins a journey for the prophet that spirals downward until he eventually finds himself at rock bottom. We are left wondering if this escape attempt is working as the ship sets off to sea. Has the prophet truly found a way to escape the presence and call of the LORD?

The following verse quickly reminds us of Psalm 139:7–12 as the psalmist cries out, "Where can I flee from your presence?" For Jonah, this beautiful Psalm turns into a nightmare as God hurls a wind against the sea, creating a mighty storm strong enough that even the boat, being personified in the story, "considered itself to be broken up." Everyone and everything in the story is filled with fear, except for Jonah. His character up to this point in the story is very intriguing. Why does he refuse his calling? Why is he seemingly at peace in the middle of a deathly storm? How is God going to respond? None of these questions is answered, at least for now, and we are left with question marks surrounding the defying prophet.

While the mariners are frantically trying to save the ship,

the story shifts to Jonah, who has descended further into the depths of the ship and fallen into a deep sleep. He is abruptly awoken by the captain of the ship, a pagan sailor, who pleads with him to get up and call out to his god. This begins another theme in the story where Jonah is constantly contrasted with the characters around him. This theme will continually cast the surrounding pagan characters in a more favorable light than the prophet of God's own nation.

Eager to discover the meaning behind this sudden storm, the sailors agreed to cast lots to find the culprit of the god's anger. Whether the lots go around and eventually reach Jonah or if they fall to him immediately, we are not told, but we are reminded again of Jonah's feeble attempt to escape the God who called him. The sailors fire off a series of questions, attempting to learn more about this unexpected traveler and the exact purpose of his mission. He rattles off a pious answer, saying he fears the LORD, creator of the heavens, earth, and sea. Ironically, he has yet to display an ounce of fear or respect for the God he claims to serve. The sailors, realizing the gravity of the situation and the God they have upset, look to Jonah for answers. Jonah finds himself in a situation where he is a mediator between these pagan sailors and God (his second opportunity to fulfill his role as prophet), and instead devises his own solution to the madness.

In what may seem like a heroic solution, Jonah offers up his own life to calm the storm. Yet, the pagan sailors refuse to offer him as a sacrifice and muster all their strength as they attempt to return to land. It is only when all efforts seem hopeless that they call out to the LORD, the God of Israel, asking that they not be held accountable for the death of the prophet. After hurling him into the sea, the story leaves a final picture of these sailors, saying, "The men feared the LORD exceedingly, and they offered a sacrifice to the LORD and made vows" (1:16).

The first contrast is complete. The prophet of God who says he fears the LORD has yet to display an ounce of that fear. Meanwhile, the pagan sailors move from a fear of the situation to a fear of God, leading them to worship. The most devout characters in the story so far turn out to be the men on the ship, and the most pagan turn out to be the prophet God has called.

Jonah's journey of descent continues as he sinks to the bottom of the sea and then is swallowed by a giant fish, where he remains for three days and three nights. We resort to giant fish simply from tradition and perhaps some deduction, but we aren't really told. It makes sense considering that there aren't many sea creatures that could store a human in their belly, but the Hebrew simply says, "giant fish." Efforts to identify the exact species that swallowed Jonah are fruitless. Even today, it is estimated that we have identified about 10% of marine species, and even that number is a guess since the total number of species is just an estimation based on what has been found. Obviously, the species known in Jonah's would be much lower, so we are left with the simple description of a large fish. It is also important to note that God "appointed" (or prepared) the fish. It doesn't say create but uses a word that means "to divide" or "set apart" for a specific task. What is significant is that the LORD's hand is involved, so miraculous efforts are not out of the question.

The belly of the fish serves as the setting for the second chapter of the book. It is here that Jonah finally addresses God after all attempts to escape have failed, even assisted suicide. In this prayer, we quickly discover that Jonah sees God's hand in all of this: "*You* cast me into the deep ... *you* brought me up from the pit." Is he casting blame on God? Or is he realizing that there simply is no escape, and he must submit? Is this a sign of repentance? He humorously contrasts himself to pagan idol worshippers (2:8), and is followed by saying that he, on the

other hand, will worship and sacrifice to God when these roles
were reversed just a few moments ago. Pious, or pretend? What
is the true heart of the prophet in the fish?

Though this prayer can be read in many different ways, it is
strikingly absent of two key ingredients: confession and repentance. We are still left wondering why he has fled in the first
place, and even more questions about his character come to the
table. He simply says, "Thank you for saving me, and I'll try to
do better." It is at this part in Jonah's story that we can sense the
most affinity for the prophet. How often do our own prayer
lives reflect that of Jonah? How often are we quick to say
"thank you" yet lack true confession and repentance, which
should serve as the pillar of our prayer life? As C.S. Lewis said
in *The Efficacy of Prayer*, "Prayer in the sense of petition, asking
for things, is a small part of it; confession and penitence are its
threshold, adoration its sanctuary, the presence and vision and
enjoyment of God its bread and wine."[4]

At the conclusion of the prayer, the LORD commands the
fish to vomit Jonah back to dry land. The third chapter opens in
a strikingly similar fashion to the beginning of the book as God
appears to Jonah again and reminds him of his task. This time
Jonah behaves more like we would expect and obeys God
without a word or comment. We are then given an odd description of the city of Nineveh. Perhaps with a bit of hyperbole, the
author emphasizes the grandeur of the city, then adds the statement that it was "a great city to/of God." Some have taken this
to be an intensifier (a super-great city) or perhaps an indication
of possession ("a great city of God's"). This phrase could also be
a figure of speech that passes over our heads due to a separation
of time and culture that we should consider and realize that we

---

4. C. S. Lewis, *The World's Last Night and Other Essays* (New York: Harper
Collins, 1952), 7.

may not be able to understand it perfectly. The addition of "three days' journey in breadth" creates even more confusion. If taken at face value, the city's dimensions would be larger than modern-day Los Angeles. A likely interpretation is that it would take Jonah three days to complete his task of proclaiming his message throughout the city. This interpretation is strengthened by the fact that it mentions Jonah had only been on one day's journey when his task was inexplicably fulfilled. Regardless, it is clear that the author wants the reader to understand that Jonah bears a difficult task both logically and, as we have seen, emotionally. Yet, to his surprise—and ours as readers—he accomplishes his mission with ease.

Contrary to his grand task, Jonah delivers a strangely brief message. In only eight words (only five words in Hebrew), he proclaims his message, "Yet forty days, and Nineveh shall be overturned." The speech gives hardly any guidance and leaves much unsaid. How are they to respond? What did they do wrong? What god is bringing this news? Who will overturn them? Perhaps Jonah doesn't really want to provide these answers, so he leaves them in the dark. Ironically, again, the Hebrew word for "overturned," which Jonah uses to mean destroyed, can also mean to change, such as a change of heart. It is this second meaning of the word that comes to life. In response to his short message, the whole city is moved to repentance, and news even reaches the king, which would be highly unlikely unless it was an extremely important message. The king then establishes a decree of confession and repentance from everyone in the city, even to the livestock. The response is almost comical, and even more so when compared to the response of Jonah in the first chapter. This wicked, evil city confesses and repents to a five-word sermon, yet Jonah is drowned in a storm, swallowed by a fish, and still refuses to repent or confess to anything.

The Hebrew word *ra'ah*, translated variously throughout the story as evil (most common), disaster, calamity, or destruction, forms a key link throughout the book (Jonah 1:2, 7, 8; 3:8, 10; 4:1, 2, 6). *Evil* is the reason for Jonah's mission in the beginning; the sailors cast lots to find answers for the *evil/disaster* that has come upon them, and the people of Nineveh repent of their *evil* way, causing God to relent in the *disaster* planned for them. In chapter 4, this word is at the center of all that has happened and will happen to Jonah.

The opening verse of chapter 4 unlocks the answer to several key questions that have come up throughout the story, as we are finally given an answer as to why Jonah fled in the beginning. The translation of this verse has been debated, with the consensus being that "Jonah was very displeased" at the situation, but this misses the point. A better translation would be something like, "and the thing was very evil to Jonah" or "and it was exceedingly evil to Jonah." Hebrew scholar Robert Alter says,

> The repetition of the term *ra'ah*, "evil," is important for the writer's purpose. When the Ninevites decide to turn away from evil, their very repentance so upsets Jonah that it becomes, ironically, an evil—which is to say, a bitter vexation for him.[5]

He is furious that God could forgive such a corrupt people.

Jonah, unable to hold in the anger that boils inside him, addresses God directly and honestly. The final chapter parallels chapter 2 in that both are prayers to God, but the substance of each prayer is very different. He says, in a way, "This is why

---

5. Robert Alter, *The Hebrew Bible: A Translation with Commentary*, vol. 2 (New York: W.W. Norton, 2019), 1297.

I fled in the first place," then he disdainfully hurls the attributes of God—attributes that are usually revered and cherished—back into God's face. Jonah says that he refused to go because he knew God would relent from the *disaster* that God said He would bring. This verse is vital to understanding the scene that follows. God will later use this moment to teach Jonah by sending *discomfort* (*ra'ah*) upon Jonah, saving him from that *discomfort*, and then exposing him again before providing a response. Jonah closes his diatribe by asking for death, which casts even more light on his intentions in the first chapter, strengthening the view that death was a selfish, rather than noble, request.

God responds to the prayer with a puzzling question, "Do you do well to be angry?" Like his response at the beginning of the book, Jonah ignores God and goes about his own business. He storms off like a child throwing a tantrum and builds himself a shelter where he will wait to see what will happen to the city. Meanwhile, the LORD appoints (same word used when appointing the fish) a castor-oil plant to provide shade for Jonah "to save him from his *discomfort*." Jonah is exceedingly joyful for the plant, but in the night, God appoints a worm to destroy the plant. He then appoints a scorching wind that causes Jonah to plead for death a third time. God repeats the question, "Do you do well to be angry?" Jonah claims that he is right and that death would be preferable to life.

Up to this point, God's actions have also been confusing. His involvement has been clear, but His intentions have been vague. Why did God want Jonah to preach to Nineveh? Why pick Jonah in the first place? Why not go to the next person in line if you really want the message delivered? Clearly, God has something He wishes to teach Jonah, and that message lies in the closing verses of the book. God uses a strange object lesson to point out the greatest piece of irony in the story: Jonah is eager to rejoice over a plant he had no control over, yet God is not allowed to have compassion for His own creation. And God leaves Jonah, and us as the reader, to sit with this question as the book ends.

Really, the book should have ended in three chapters. The story closes with the prophet overcoming himself to deliver a message to his enemies as he rides off into the sunset. Chapter 4 only complicates the story. But it is within this final chapter that the true meaning of the book is revealed. What exactly is God trying to teach Jonah through all of this? And since it is also a message for Israel, what is God trying to teach His people? The story tests the limits of God's grace and mercy.

But who exactly deserves God's grace and mercy? If you asked Israel at this time, they would likely say that they deserve it. The book of Jonah comes to challenge that answer. What makes you deserving of such a gift? Is it something you've done, or is it simply because you have been chosen by God? And what exactly sets you apart from all your neighbors? Are you any more deserving than they? The mirror then gets held up to the reader. What have we done to deserve God's grace and mercy? The book of Romans quickly comes to mind,

> For while we were still weak, at the right time Christ died for the ungodly. For one will scarcely die for a righteous person— though perhaps for a good person one would dare even to die —but God shows his love for us in that while we were still sinners, Christ died for us (Romans 5:6–8).

We, like Israel, like Jonah, were in a position of hopelessness. It is only by the grace of God that we can have life with Him.

In this way, the book serves as the perfect prologue to the prophetic period as Jonah becomes a microcosm of God's people who also struggle to live up to their calling. But God's mercy is not the only factor. Mercy must be balanced by justice. God's dealings with Nineveh will foreshadow His relationship with Israel. Though God extends a compassionate hand to Ninevah now, the book of Nahum will foretell its destruction. In an eerily similar fashion, Jeremiah will later warns Judah by saying, "Behold, I am shaping disaster against you and devising a plan against you. Return, everyone from his evil way, and amend your ways and your deeds" (Jeremiah 18:11). Just as Nineveh is not isolated from the mercy of God, so Israel and Judah are not immune to God's justice. Their sins will eventually catch up to them, leading to the destruction and exile of both Samaria and Jerusalem. This balance is constantly on display throughout the prophets as God continually walks the line between mercy and justice for His people and the nations around them.

Reflection Questions

1. We often think of fear as a negative thing, but the biblical writers (Old and New Testament) include fear as an important part of one's faith. Why is that the case? What role does fear play in faith? Has fear played a role in your own faith?

2. Is Jonah a good guy or a bad guy? Are there any other biblical characters that remind you of Jonah? Do you see any similarities between yourself and Jonah?

3. What is the point of this book? Clearly, it isn't just trying to tell an interesting story. Why does God send Jonah through all of this? What is the message God is trying to send to His people?

4. In what ways do we run from our responsibility as Christians, like Jonah ran from his prophetic call?
5. In what ways does God balance justice and mercy throughout the biblical story?
6. "Jonah becomes a microcosm of God's people." In what ways does Jonah's life parallel the stories of Israel and Judah?

Chapter 3

The Book of Amos

Complacency is a deadly foe of all spiritual growth. Acute desire must be present or there will be no manifestation of Christ to His people. He waits to be wanted. Too bad that with many of us He waits so long, so very long, in vain.[1]

— A.W. Tozer, *The Pursuit of God: The Human Thirst for the Divine*

IN THE BOOK OF JONAH, it is the characters in the story who force us to reflect and examine ourselves. We are left to compare ourselves to the stubborn prophet and the repentant pagans. For Amos, his rhetoric will force reflection upon both the reader and the wayward, complacent nation of Israel. Israel is still living comfortable, prosperous, and peaceful lives under the reign of Jeroboam II, but much of that will change as political, spiritual, and military woes are on the horizon. For now, at

---

1. A.W. Tozer, *The Pursuit of God* (Harrisburg, PA: Christian Publications, 1948), 17.

least, they sit untroubled in their summer and winter houses, laden with ivory (3:14), abusing their privileged position among the nations. The prophet Amos gets thrust into the picture to forcefully disrupt this nation's way of life and urge them to turn back to God. Despite his most desperate efforts, God's own people refuse to listen to His message (the exact opposite of the wicked city of Nineveh in the book of Jonah). As a result, the Day of the LORD, a day of God's "unmistakable and powerful intervention,"[2] will soon come for God's own people as the surrounding nations sit and watch.

The book opens with the LORD roaring from Zion—His holy mountain—down to the inhabitants below, and the whole land quakes in His presence. A key refrain is repeated throughout the opening chapter, "for three transgressions...and for four," as God calls out the sins of the surrounding nations. This begins the first section of the book (chs. 1–2), where God pronounces judgment on all the nations of the earth. The structure of the section is perhaps just as important to Amos' message as the content. Looking at a map, Amos goes in a spiral pattern around Israel, starting with the most distant nation of Damascus to the north, moving to Gaza of the Philistines to the southwest coast, and then to Tyre of the Phoenicians on the northwest coast. These are all foreign nations, and each has presented problems for Israel in the past. In the eyes of Israel, God's disapproval of these foreigners comes as no surprise, and they likely begin rejoicing in the judgment that befalls their enemies. As Amos swiftly moves through his list, Israel sinks comfortably into their chair, listening to the destruction that their surrounding enemies will soon endure. In the second set of nations, the swirl pattern gets a little tighter as Amos quickly

---

2. J.D. Barker, "Day of the Lord," *DOTP* (Downers Grove: InterVarsity Press, 2012), 132.

shifts from the Edomites in the south to the Ammonites in the east, Moab in the southwest, and finishes with Judah directly to the south. Each of these nations is a distant relative of Israel, with Judah being both neighbor and brother to the northern kingdom. The audience grows increasingly uncomfortable as Amos moves closer and closer to home.

If you pick up a commentary on Amos, you will notice that there is a lot of discussion surrounding the phrase "for three transgressions ... and for four." Some see it as just a common idiom, some claim we should expect four or seven sins to be listed, and others allude to the significance of the number seven, which carries the idea of completion (either in God's patience or as the pinnacle of their sinful activity). It is hard to know exactly, but there does seem to be an element of incompleteness in each of the oracles. That is what stands out the most in this opening section. Only one or two sins are listed, a punishment is given, and then on to the next nation. He moves through each nation with haste, perhaps suggesting that the real target of God's anger lies elsewhere.[3] Like Jonah, Amos also carries a message of warning, but to whom is it directed?

The second chapter contains the climax of Amos's speech as the spiral pattern ends with Israel, who receives the most exhaustive rebuke. While the surrounding nations were limited to either one or two sins and a punishment, Israel received the full force of the "for three transgressions ... and for four" as God called out their greed, mistreatment of the poor, idol worship, and lack of commitment. As a result, judgment will come, and all the sources of strength and security they rely on shall fail them (Amos 2:13–16). Even the mightiest of their troops will go away naked and ashamed on that day (2:16).

---

3. Robert B. Chisholm, *Handbook on the Prophets* (Grand Rapids: Baker Academic, 2002), 379.

"You only have I known of all the families of the earth; therefore, I will punish you for all your iniquities" (Amos 3:2). God begins His message with a tone of disappointment. Israel, God's chosen people, His own nation that He delivered from slavery and established in a fruitful land, was meant to be a light among the nations. Not only have they failed to be that light, but they have also abused their privileged position and turned away from all that God has asked of them. Israel's chosenness was meant to be the cornerstone of their faith and a refuge in dark times. The prophets began to see that Israel had abused their chosenness and forsaken who they were meant to be. "They had to remind the people that chosenness must not be mistaken as divine favoritism or immunity from chastisement, but, on the contrary, that it meant being more seriously exposed to divine judgement and chastisement."[4] The third chapter begins the second major section in Amos (chs. 3–6), elaborating on the sin and coming punishment of Israel. After calling out Israel's neglect, he details the disaster to come, emphasizing that it is a result of God's own hand. This will be a key theme throughout the prophets as they remind the people that the coming exile and destruction of the nation is a result of God's punishment for His people. They reinforce that Israel's fate is not in the hands of Assyria or Babylon but in the hands of God.

This idea of God punishing His people is hard to grasp, and even Amos himself struggles with this idea throughout the book. In contrast to the Ninevites of Jonah's story, who were given a chance of repentance because "they did not know their left hand from their right," Israel has been given the law and told what God wants, yet they repeatedly turn away from Him. While other prophets (especially Hosea) will focus more on the

---

4. Heschel, *Prophets*, 39.

collision and balance between God's judgment and God's mercy, the book of Amos will focus primarily on the reason and necessity of God's judgment. God cannot sit idly by as violence overtakes the hearts of His people. As Terrence Fretheim writes, "Wrath and violence are not divine attributes, but responses to creaturely sin, indeed the sins of violence."[5] Yes, God is a God of mercy, but He is also just and will not turn a blind eye to continual corruption and sin, especially among His own people.

* * *

Window into the Social Corruption within Israel

There are signs of a progressive disintegration of the structure of Israelite society, and of a harsh system that tended to place the poor at the mercy of the rich. The former, forced in hard times to borrow from the latter at usurious rates of interest, mortgaging their land, if not their own persons or those of their children, in security, faced—and, one gathers, not infrequently (II Kings 4:1)—the prospect of eviction, if not slavery.[6]

To highlight how far Israel has fallen from God, Amos calls the Philistine and Egyptian nations to assemble on the mountains and watch as God punishes His people. The exact purpose of assembling them is not entirely clear. Is he saying that these nations are morally superior? Is he calling the nations to bear witness as God brings Israel to court? Is it a rhetorical device

---

5. Michael J. Chan and Brent A. Strawn, eds., *What Kind of God?: Collected Essays of Terrence Fretheim* (Winona Lake: Eisenbrauns, 2015), 134.
6. John Bright, *A History of Israel*, 3rd ed. (Philadelphia: Westminster Press, 1981), 244.

used to further offend the Israelites? It is likely that all these possibilities are in play as Amos seems to talk directly to the nations and then back to Israel as if they are all there listening to him. The result, however, is clear. Israel will be plundered by an adversary, and only a small remnant will be salvaged (vv. 11–12). The horns of the altar (the place where fugitives seeking asylum would hold on to) will be cut off, making it clear that Israel will not find protection from God's coming judgment.[7]

* * *

Chapter 4 opens with a picture of Israel's women—who have been lazily engorging themselves while simultaneously oppressing the poor among them—being driven away with fishing hooks. These opening verses give a window into the harsh practice of exile that Israel will soon experience. The bulk of the chapter (vv 6–13) consists of a long series of hardships that God claims to have brought upon the people. This section raises some fairly difficult questions. Is it fair that God does this to His people? Does God still do this to His people? We easily recognize blessings as being given by the Lord, but are we comfortable with the idea of God taking them away? Before going too far, it is important to note that we shouldn't take passages like this out of context and build a whole theology around them. These passages need to be treated in a similar way to passages stating how God will bless His people if they follow Him. While it is true that God blesses His people, there is a way to take these passages too far and fall into a prosperity gospel where we claim that following God must mean we become financially blessed as a result. God is often seen testing

---

7. Chisholm, *Handbook*, 388.

His people both in abundance and in absence, but there is always a purpose behind the action, a goal beyond mere blessings and hardships.

The closing line in each of these verses reveals what God truly desires. He desires our hearts. In this section, we see God doing all He can to pull the hearts of His people back to Himself—hearts that have fallen far away from the God they once served. It is often hardships and trials that wake us up and cause us to reach out to God. As C.S. Lewis once wrote, "God whispers to us in our pleasures, speaks in our conscience, but shouts in our pains: it is His megaphone to rouse a deaf world."[8] Here we find the Israelites in a dreadful situation; neither blessing nor hardship will turn their calloused hearts to God. They are left to rely on the gods of their own hands.

Chapter 5 begins with God saying, "Hear the *qinah* I intone concerning you, O Israel." The Hebrew word *qinah* is used frequently in Jeremiah and Ezekiel and is often translated as "lament," but also as "funeral song," "weeping," or "mourning." But who is the funeral song for? Who has fallen? For whom do we mourn? The following verse of the song answers, "Fallen, no more to rise, is the virgin Israel; forsaken on her land, with none to raise her up." God speaks as if He is presiding over the funeral of a nation already passed. Yet, there is still hope. Throughout the chapter, the prophet implores Israel to return, saying three different times, "seek God and live" (vv. 4, 6, and 14). "Harsh is God's intolerance of injustice, but the gate of repentance remains open."[9] The final plea in 5:14–15 is eerily similar to the wording of Jonah (1:6; 3:9), "seek good, and not evil, that you may live ... it may be that the

---

8. C. S. Lewis, *The Problem of Pain*, in *The C.S. Lewis Signature Classics* (New York: Harper Collins, 2017), 604.

9. Heschel, *Prophets*, 43.

LORD, the God of hosts, will be gracious to the remnant of Joseph." Yet again, contrary to the Ninevites, the people ignore the words of the prophet. The funeral goes on.

In the last section of chapter 5, the Day of the LORD—a day that was expected to be the moment of salvation for Israel when her enemies would be destroyed—is flipped on its head. To all those who thought that simply being God's chosen people is enough for salvation, judgment has come. After listing the details of that day, God renounced their sacrifices and festivals, which were the core of the Israelite religion. You can almost hear the reply of the people after Amos commands them to seek God, "What do you mean, seek God? We sacrifice, we worship at the temple, we do seek God every day!" Though they offered sacrifices, they did not truly seek Him. Though they go daily to the temple, they do not truly worship. Here lies one of the most challenging parts of the Christian faith: the ability to truly combine heart and worship.

Maybe we are often guilty of entering into worship with the expectation that the heart will automatically follow. We want to experience God, so we "enter into worship." This mindset isn't necessarily wrong, but the biblical story often paints a different picture of true worship. We frequently meet characters who fall down and worship as an overflow of the heart. Hannah, after being given news of a son, begins her prayer, "My heart rejoices in the LORD" (1 Samuel 2:1). Mary, after receiving news of Jesus, responds in an identical way in Luke's gospel. But rejoicing isn't the only emotion of a worshipful heart. In times of hardship, the Psalmist, out of the agony in his heart, cries, "As the deer pants for the water brooks, so my soul pants for you, O God" (Psalm 42:1). Christ, in His final moments alone and in anguish, falls down before His Father and prays, "Not my will, but yours be done."

To seek God, we take our hearts, in whatever state they

may be, and pour them out before our creator. Worship is not a cure but a response; a response to all that life throws our way. Again, this is one of the most difficult aspects of the Christian faith, so this is not a perfect recipe. The distinction is important, though, because the opposite (entering into worship as a way to pull the heart to God) risks making ourselves the center of worship rather than God. Maybe this is what John Bunyan was getting at when he said, "In prayer it is better to have a heart without words than words without a heart."[10]

Israel, however, has failed to seek God, and their hearts clearly lie elsewhere, resulting in a complete futility of all their worship. The feasts and gatherings are rejected, God turns a blind eye to their sacrifices, and all their songs of worship become a noisy commotion to God's ears. Chapter 5 closes with another warning of the exile that will soon come. God reinforces His point about worship as He reminds Israel of their time in the wilderness. The Israelite faith, at its core, was not about feasts and sacrifices but about God leading His people through the dangerous wilderness and into the land of promise. The prophets will continually look back at the wilderness wanderings as a reminder of what's really important—the relationship between God and Israel.

Even with all these intense declarations of judgment, chapter 6 begins with a picture of Israel sitting in their ivory homes, unfazed by the warnings they hear. Interestingly, these houses that Amos keeps mentioning (6:4–7) come up again after exile in the words of Haggai, the prophet who accuses Israel of being quick to build back their own homes after returning from exile but neglecting to build the House of the LORD. The apathetic hearts of the people are continuously on display throughout the prophets, even after exile. Here in

---

10. John Bunyan, *The Poetry of John Bunyan*, vol. 1 (Portable Poetry, 2017).

Amos 6, not only does apathy plague the people, but in their comfort, they also "bring near the seat of violence" and are unconcerned about the spiritual corruption happening among them. These people who sit comfortably now will be "the first of those who go into exile." Those who are left will walk about in fear, hiding from the God who has handed them over to destruction (vv. 9–10).

Chapters 7–9 (excluding a small closing section at the end of the book) make up the final section of Amos's prophecy. Chapter 7 begins with a series of visions God reveals to the prophet, each indicated by the line, "This is what the Lord God showed me ..." (7:1, 4, 7; 8:1 ESV). The first three pictures are a coming disaster upon the nation. Amos pleads with God to hold back His judgment, recalling images of Moses and Abraham interceding on behalf of the people. A short story is then inserted into the chapter, showing the people's rejection of Amos, prompting him to pronounce judgment and exile upon the nation. This short episode causes Amos to experience first-hand the corruption of the people he was just defending.

The final vision in chapter 8 is built around a keyword play to highlight the ultimate message that God intends to teach Amos. God shows Amos a basket of summer fruit (Hebrew: *qayits*), which he quickly identifies. God then says that the end (Hebrew: *qeyts*) has come upon Israel. This is the same word used in Genesis 6:13 when God initiates the destruction of the world, saying that "the end (*qeyts*) of all flesh has come before me." He then says, "I will never again pass by them." The Hebrew word for "pass by" has multiple possible meanings: "to pass through/over someone," "to become involved with some-one," or "to pass over transgressions (i.e., to forgive)."[11] It seems likely, especially considering the following verses, that this

---

11. Ludwig Koehler, et.al, "עבר" *HALOT*, 778.

word was chosen to incorporate all three possible meanings. The LORD will no longer spare the nation. As a result, their songs of joy will become wailings (same word used in ch 5), judgment will come, and Israel will experience a famine of God's words.

This famine becomes painfully real as there is a period of silence in the history of God's people where they hear no word from God. This is commonly referred to as the Intertestamental period (or "Second Temple Period," the gap between the Old and New Testaments), where God's people are left without any direct contact with God through appearances or prophets. However, like the book of Esther, though God does not speak, He is still working in the background. The people do not hear again until the coming of Christ, where John says that "the Word of God became flesh and dwelt among us."

In the final chapter, the wrath prepared for the Day of the Lord is poured out against Israel. There is nowhere to hide from God as He sets out against Israel, who have become like the foreign, unclean nations of Cush and Philistine before Him. Yet, there is still hope for those who are faithful. The house of Jacob will be restored. The future vision of hope given in the closing verses pictures Israel as a united nation planted securely in a fruitful land. This gives the later exilic community a picture of hope to hold on to while in captivity. Currently, however, the divided nation is unaffected by the moral corruption within their own city gates (perhaps the reason Amos begins in the way it does by condemning surrounding nations first) and will remain that way despite Amos's heartfelt preaching.

Amos is not a comfortable book to read, and that is on purpose. He is endowed with the task of waking up a cold and unrepentant nation before it's too late. To do that, extreme language and imagery are used, but to no avail. His heavy message highlights the seriousness of sin both in the individual and in the community. For Amos, there is no middle ground in faith. Either we are wholeheartedly seeking God, or we are complacently allowing sin to go unchecked in our lives. The heart never sits still. It always moves toward something. If not toward God, then it grows hard and calloused. Amos's hope is to reach the people before their hearts grow impenetrable.

Reflection Questions

1. In our section on "What manner of man is the prophet," which of the 10 did you see most clearly in Amos?

2. Amos talks often about how God deals with His people. What are some similarities between how God dealt with Israel and how He deals with us today?

3. What role does the heart play in worship for Amos? How does that challenge the way you view or approach worship?

4. What are some things we can do to better prepare our hearts for worship? What are some mistakes we can make in approaching worship?

5. In the opening quote, Tozer said that "complacency is the deadly foe of all spiritual growth." Do you agree with him? How have you seen complacency affect your own spiritual life?

Chapter 4

The Book of Hosea

The crux of the matter is, of course, the question of forgiveness. Forgetting is something that time alone takes care of, but forgiveness is an act of volition, and only the sufferer is qualified to make the decision.[1]

— Simon Wiesenthal, *The Sunflower: On the Possibilities and Limits of Forgiveness*

"THE CONTRAST between Amos and Hosea is seen both in what they condemn and in what they stress. To Amos, the principal sin is *injustice*; to Hosea, it is *idolatry*. Amos inveighs against evil *deeds*; Hosea attacks the absence of *inwardness*."[2] Simon Wiesenthal's book, *The Sunflower*, focuses on the burdensome task of forgiveness. After facing one of the most difficult decisions of his life, he chooses to reject the path of

---

1. Simon Wiesenthal, *The Sunflower: On the Possibilities and Limits of Forgiveness*, rev. ed. (New York: Schocken Books, 1997), 97–8.
2. Heschel, *Prophets*, 74.

forgiveness and has been haunted by his decision ever since. He then invites the reader into his own story as a Jew taken from a concentration camp and brought before a dying SS guard seeking mercy and asks, "Would you grant him forgiveness?" A simple topic becomes a seemingly impossible question.

The nation of Israel is repeatedly guilty of taking God's grace and mercy for granted. Confidence in God's grace can quickly become complacency in God's grace if we are not constantly mindful of the cross. The cross, while reminding us of the reality of our own sin, also reveals the depths of God's love. The reality of sin and the love of God are powerfully on display in Hosea as he gives us a window into the inner life of God. Much like Wiesenthal's story, in Hosea, we aren't just told about the fact of God's forgiveness, but we are given a first-hand look at just how difficult the path of forgiveness can be for the one who is wronged.

The book of Hosea is extremely unique and fairly challenging in many respects. It contains a complicated structure and use of language that can make it difficult to follow at times. Keeping the big picture in mind helps make sense of the details as you move through the book. Hosea is the collision point of two extremely powerful forces: the continual sin of Israel and the deep love/compassion of God (Hebrew: *hesed*). What happens when these powerful forces collide? Which side proves stronger, love or justice? Hosea employs extremely strong language and bold imagery to show the immense power of these two forces. Stuck in the middle of these opposing forces is a God who is torn between a desire to love and protect His children and a realization that they will not stop running away until they truly understand the depths of their sin.

The main theme in the book is Israel's lack of a "knowledge of God." Understanding the intricacies of this theme will help make sense of the language and imagery used throughout the book. When we think of knowledge, our minds default to more of an analytical definition; we know information about people, places, and things. Knowledge in the biblical world operated very differently, possessing a wider range of meanings than our typical understanding.

> In most Semitic languages, [knowledge] signifies sexual union as well as mental and spiritual activity ... more than possession of abstract concepts, knowledge encompasses inner appropriation, feeling, a reception into the soul ... both an intellectual and emotional act.[3]

Heschel goes on to list five different stories in Israel's history where this phrase "to know" transcends our modern understanding: God seeing Israel's hardships in slavery (Exodus 2:24–25), knowing through experience (Exodus 23:9), having or lacking a close connection to someone (Exodus 1:8), having or lacking reverence (1 Samuel 2:12), and the relations between husband and wife (Genesis 4:1).[4] It is a word that means involvement with, longing for, and commitment to something or someone. Israel will be constantly charged with lacking knowledge of God. Instead, they have come to know the gods of the nations around them—gods that have been integrated into Israel's worship over time.

The book is going to flow in and out of 3 main topics (sometimes very abruptly): sin/rebellion, judgment, and return/renewal. Idolatry has plagued the nation, and Hosea will lay that sin before Israel in a very vivid way. As a result of the sin filling His nation, God has no choice but to act and judge His people.

---

3. Heschel, *Prophets*, 70.
4. Heschel, *Prophets*, 71–2.

Again, we are faced with the challenging topic of God's judgment. As you encounter these sections, it may be helpful to keep this quote by Terrence Fretheim in mind: "Thinking of God as judge, remember that the judge behind the bench is the spouse of the accused one in the dock."[5] This will become increasingly clear throughout the book of Hosea as God knows the people must be judged for their sins, yet He still looks on with compassion for His creation. That leads to the final topic of renewal. The story will frequently cut to images and promises of a future hope to come for those who return to Him. The overwhelming picture in the prophets is that judgment is not the end of God's relationship with His people.

The Political Situation of Hosea's Time

Although Assyria had been in a period of weakness for some time, their resurgence was just on the horizon. Around 744 BCE, there arose a new leader in Assyria, named Tiglath-Pileser III, who revived Assyria's influence and began re-establishing control throughout the Middle East. Around 738 BCE, he began to push into the Palestinian region, forcing local kings to fight or pay tribute to Assyria. Israel, under King Menahem, was among the nations to pay tribute (likely due to Israel's weakened status through infighting and political corruption after the death of Jeroboam II), which is recorded in 2 Kings 15:19–20. While it offered them momentary protection, heavy local taxes and life under the shadow of a dominant foreign nation were not conditions that kept the people happy. These political circumstances would further infuriate the people and

---

5. Chan and Strawn, *Collected Essays*, 146.

eventually lead to a coalition between Syria and Israel, which set the stage for the coming Syro-Ephraimite War. This conflict will play a huge role in the downfall of Israel and contains an important historical tie to the book of Isaiah.

* * *

Both the flow of these main topics and the "knowledge of God" theme are woven into the narrative of the first three chapters of Hosea. Properly understanding these chapters will help interpret the rest of the book (and the prophetic period in general). Hosea's prophetic career begins in a unique way. In a rather odd command, Hosea is told by God to marry a "wife of whoredom" and to have "children of whoredom" before he ever begins his ministry. This chapter has been the battleground of numerous debates as scholars try to explain the oddities within these opening chapters. We will touch on some of those issues below, but at the onset, we must be reminded to keep the big picture in view: how does a loving God respond to a wayward people? The story of Hosea and Gomer is a direct parallel to the relationship between God and Israel. God, like Hosea, is married to an unfaithful spouse, Israel. I know, for many people, infidelity can be a difficult subject to talk about. We should understand, though, that the subject of adultery is not chosen flippantly. Quite the opposite, the subject is chosen to highlight just how important the covenant is to God and to provide a first-hand look into the pain God feels when abandoned by His people. God loves His people truly and deeply. His love is one that our minds cannot truly comprehend. And His pain, when abandoned, is just as deep as His love. God uses the strongest of human relationships to help us understand the abandonment He endures. He seeks to give us a window into His own sorrow.

* * *

Textual Questions in Hosea 1

There are several debates surrounding the story of Hosea and Gomer's marriage. Rather than detouring at each one in the comments, a summary of the key debates will be listed here. The vague nature of each of these topics has led to much speculation on behalf of scholars trying to determine the precise meaning of each term. In most cases, it is best to leave the ambiguity and accept that the exact meaning is lost in time. We detour here, not to find answers but to have a better understanding of the discussion around each problem. With each of these, it is important not to get lost in the details. We must remember that Hosea's marriage is merely the vehicle for the main theme, which is God's relationship with Israel.

"Wife of whoredom" — This phrase is rather odd and probably the most speculative of the first chapter. If Hosea was told to marry a prostitute specifically, the expected phrase would be "marry a woman of prostitution," but he is told to take a "wife of prostitution." Does this mean she is a prostitute? Is she just known for her bad reputation? Is this foreshadowing to show that she will become unfaithful? Unfortunately, the text doesn't answer any of these questions. Perhaps the text is highlighting that not only is Hosea being asked to go and take a prostitute, but this prostitute will be his wife. Even with all the ambiguity, the main point is clear: Hosea will marry a woman who will not be faithful to him, just as Israel has not been faithful to God.

"Children of whoredom" — Questions are raised because the ESV and other translations say, "have children ..." but the Hebrew text doesn't say "have," it just says take a wife and children ..." This causes many to question if these children are in fact Hosea's or if this is evidence of Gomer's unfaithfulness to Hosea. Again, the text remains unclear except for Jezreel, who is specifically mentioned as being born to Hosea. It seems likely that the following kids are implied to be Hosea's, but there remains room for that too not be the case.

Moral question of Hosea marrying Gomer — Many commentators throughout history have been bothered by the fact that God would command Hosea to marry (and then remarry) such a sinful woman. This has caused some to read the story as an allegory or vision, but the moral repugnance of the command is what makes the book so powerful. You are immediately forced to ask, "Why would God command such a thing?" And the painful answer given is, "Because you (Israel) have cheated on your spouse (God)." Any attempt to shy away from this misses the main theme of the book.

Hosea is first commanded to go and take a "wife of whoredom" and to have "children of whoredom" with her. The command is intentionally odd and controversial. Immediately, you begin to ask, "Why would God do something like this?" The answer is given quickly as God gives a reason for the odd command, saying, "for the land commits great whoredom by forsaking the LORD" (1:2). Here, the nation is confronted with their adultery. The parallels are set in place as the marriage between Hosea and Gomer will represent the relationship between God and Israel. The couple soon has their first child, and Hosea names him Jezreel (Hebrew: "to scatter"), which begins a series of symbolic names for each of their children. This name is meant to remind Israel of the violence that took place in the Valley of Jezreel when Jehu spilled blood to overthrow King Omri's dynasty (1 Kings 9–10).

The clarifying phrase after naming Jezreel in the ESV, "I will punish the house of Jehu for the blood of Jezreel," sounds misleading. After all, it was God who commanded that Jehu take the throne from Joram. The matter is further complicated when God gives His seal of approval after the violent affair is completed (2 Kings 10:28–31). It is perhaps better to read this verse as "I will bring the bloodshed of Jezreel upon the house of Jehu."[6] Instead of a judgment against the actions of Jehu, the statement shows that the violent and bloody end of the Omride dynasty in Jezreel will recur again in Hosea's day upon the future succession of kings. This prophecy will come to life after the powerful reign of Jeroboam II, as five different kings rise and fall in a span of only 20 years. In most of these stories, the throne is taken by violence, bloodshed, and political deception.

Gomer becomes pregnant again, but the text simply says, "bore a daughter" without specifically naming Hosea as the father. Some commentators see this as an intentional omission, claiming that the father is not Hosea, while others are strongly opposed, saying that the story implies Hosea is the father. The text is vague and doesn't provide a firm answer either way, but the omission is suspicious and perhaps meant to make us question Gomer's faithfulness to Hosea. This child receives the symbolic name Lo-Ruhama (Hebrew: "no mercy"), and once she is weaned, another child is born in the same way, with the text again omitting the details of the father's identity. This child is named Lo-Ammi (Hebrew: "not my people") because the people have broken the covenant. As a result, the relationship that was formed through that covenant has now come to an end (setting the scene for Jeremiah's promise of a new covenant to come).

---

6. Duane A. Garrett. *Hosea, Joel*, The New American Commentary, vol. 19A (Nashville: Broadman & Holman, 1997), 57.

Amid all the heartbreak, there remains a flash of hope. The closing verses of the chapter contain the first major shift in tone as a future hope steals the scene to remind the people that this rejection by God is not final. There will be a day when Israel and Judah will be gathered again, "for great will be the day of Jezreel." The Hebrew word used for the first child can have both a positive and a negative connotation. The first usage in verse 4 is negative ("scatter"), but the word primarily means "to sow" (as in scattering seed in a field to grow), which carries more of a positive connotation. God plays on the meanings of the children's names to show that Israel's fate will soon be reversed. This is also the first of many instances where Hosea uses plant/desert imagery to show Israel's fruitful future compared to their current corruption.

Chapter two delves into the sin of Gomer (Israel) in even more detail. Hosea is pictured pleading with his children to help pull their mother back after she has strayed away. Verse 3 uses vivid imagery to show how God will punish her, which is also used to foreshadow Israel's looming exile. The big picture is summed up in 2:13: Israel has left God to pursue other gods. While the bulk of chapter 2 has been about sin and judgment, verse 14 provides another glimpse into the future where God's mercy floods the scene. The empty, deserted wilderness that Israel has created will soon be turned into a beautiful oasis. The covenant will be renewed as in "the days of Israel's youth," and on that day, God will take back Israel so that He alone will be their God. "I will betroth you to me in faithfulness. And you shall *know* the LORD" (Hosea 2:20).

The marriage of Hosea and Gomer takes a similar turn in chapter 3 as God commands him to "go and love again" a woman who has given herself to another man. The wording of these opening verses is vague, and many have used the ambiguity to conclude that Hosea is commanded to go and love a different woman, not Gomer. If that is true, the living illustration of the opening chapter seems to crumble. God is trying to demonstrate His love for an unfaithful Israel. To do so, He sends Hosea to love again his unfaithful spouse. The wording of this verse, combined with everything that has come before, leaves us without a doubt that Gomer (and, by analogy, Israel) has committed adultery and forsaken her husband. That is the whole point. God is forcing Israel to confront their own sin. The story repeatedly reminds you just how unfaithful this woman is to reflect the adulterous heart of Israel. Yet, God tells Hosea to take her back. "Go and love again" is God's response. "Just as the LORD loves Israel."

This whole passage is the way in which Hosea is to "love" his wife. This is a glimpse into the type of love that God has for His people. Why is God doing all this to Hosea? There are two reasons, one negative and one positive. The first reason is to make Israel's sin real. Hosea and the people needed to experience firsthand the pain that sin causes in relationships. They have become numb to their side of the relationship, so they need to feel the pain of an abandoned partner. That is the negative side. The second reason is to paint a tangible picture of God's love for His people. How exactly does God love us? This story shows love in action. God fought abandonment and heartbreak to take back the one He loves. This is the positive side, and this is the love that we are reminded of in the New Testament (Ephesians 2:1–10; Colossians 2:6–15; 1 John 3:1, 16–24).

He then goes and purchases his wife back from her pagan temple and reminds her of the commitment they once had to one another. For many days, she must "sit/live with Hosea," meaning she must no longer search after other men but learn to give herself fully to her husband to renew the lost bond. This is one of the many instances in the Bible where forgiveness and mercy are not just seen as a gift, but a challenge. I think of Peter sitting along the shore eating fish with the risen Christ whom he had just denied (John 21:15–19). Through a simple question, Jesus makes Peter confront his sin. Then, alongside forgiveness, Jesus offers a challenge. He warns him of the difficult road ahead and then says, "Follow me." What is true for Peter is true for Gomer and true for us. We have been given grace and mercy far beyond what we deserve, and now the challenge becomes, "What will you do with the new life you have been given?"

Chapters 4–14 make up a new section that will flow between the main topics of sin, judgment, and renewal while also making use of all the themes and phrases used in the first three chapters. Chapters 4–6 hit on each of the main themes individually by revealing Israel's sin (ch. 4), announcing judgment (ch. 5), and providing hope (6:1–3). The rest of the book will not flow as neatly, but the overall pattern will remain. In chapter 4, the sins of the people are listed in vivid detail. There is no truth, loyalty, or knowledge of God in the land. The more that was given to them, the more they fell away, allowing other gods to fill their worship. Yet, Judah is singled out as not having fallen into the same trap as Israel and is told to stay clean of Israel's sinfulness.

Chapter 5 speaks more directly to the priests, the leaders of the nation, holding them accountable for the downward turn of the nation. Because they align themselves against God, they have made God their enemy and must face the punishment as a result. Toward the end of the chapter (5:13) we see the first of many instances where Israel is called out for seeking security and wealth from nations around them instead of trusting in God which will eventually bring about their downfall (cf. 7:8–11; 8:7–10; 9:3; 11:5–7; 12:1; 14:3). The final verse in chapter 5 sets us up for a small section of hope as Hosea begins to plead with his people to turn back to the LORD who is still good and faithful to them. Chapter 6 closes by picturing God as a parent torn between what to do with their wayward children. Similar images will come up throughout the remainder of the book, giving a window into the heart of God as He continues to be torn between judgment and compassion (cf. 11:8–9; 13:1–3). It's like a scene in a movie where the character talks to himself as if someone were there listening. "All I wanted was your heart, Israel, but you betrayed me" (6:6–7). Even Gilead and Shechem, which were cities of sanctuary and refuge from evil in the time of the Judges (Joshua 20:1–8), are now filled with murder and bloodshed—there is no place safe from the violence within the nation.

Chapter 7 begins a long stretch alternating between sin and punishment, while the anticipated section of hope and renewal will not show up until Chapter 11. Their evil has engulfed them (7:2), and they have reached a time of weakness. Instead of turning to God, they "gnash themselves" (perhaps a form of self-mutilation in Canaanite worship[7]) and seek help from other nations around them (vv. 14–16). This constant turning to other nations will quickly weaken Israel (8:7–10), and soon their political and spiritual realms will become desolate. Throughout the section, we are frequently reminded of the relationship at its pure beginning, and that it was Israel, not God, who violated and destroyed the covenant (9:10). Again, the prophets emphasize the singular cause for the coming exile, sin.

Chapter 9 is difficult to read in many aspects, but especially when God mentions the loss of children in vv 11–12. The language is extremely strong, but it should be remembered that, for a nation, no children is also a way of saying no future.

---

7. Chisholm, *Handbook*, 356.

Perhaps this can be read as a graphically poetic way of threatening Israel's sudden and violent end. Chapter 10 continues the dark imagery by depicting the death and destruction that the coming exile will bring. The high places—which were altars created for the worship of other gods, especially prevalent during the reign of Jeroboam—would be destroyed, and soon weeds would cover the pile of wreckage as the nation would be stripped of their land.

Chapter 11 finally breaks away from the judgment and sin cycle into a message of hope, but that message doesn't last long. The opening verses (11:1–4) again paint God as a loving parent who raised and nurtured His child only to have them walk away. They wandered into the arms of other nations and rejected the God of their childhood. This will be the cause of their destruction as another nation will swoop in and overtake them. But this will not be the final word for God and Israel. After another deliberation between judgment and mercy, God vows to bring back His people from exile and comfort them once more (vv. 8–11). Chapter 12 recalls the story of Jacob from the book of Genesis. Jacob, who once relied on deception to get his way, finally encountered God and turned to Him. Israel must do the same in order to survive. "So you, by the help of your God, return, hold fast to love and justice, and wait continually for your God" (Hosea 12:6).

Chapter 13 begins with a picture of Israel's former influence among the nations: "when they spoke, there was trembling." They were once a people whom many feared and respected, but their sin destroyed their influence. Now they will disappear like the morning mist or chaff driven by the wind (cf. Psalm 1).[8] After being reminded of what God has done for

---

8. Cf. Hosea 6, where the morning mist is used to show the consistency of God's loyalty and love. This is a prime example of how Hosea and the other

them, they are told again of the destruction that lies ahead. The God who fought for them will now fight against them. The two opening lines in verse 14 seem oddly hopeful and shift tone quicker than expected. Many versions have these verses as statements, but they could also be read as a question, which seems more appropriate considering the context. "Shall I ransom them from the power of Sheol? Shall I redeem them from death?" Where earlier God was hesitant to judge because of compassion, here God is hesitant to have compassion because of the constant rejection of Israel. The decision has been made, "Samaria shall bear her guilt."

The final chapter ends with the longest message of hope in the entire book. It takes the form of a plea by Hosea to return to God. They are told to repent, turn away from trusting in Assyria and worshipping gods made with their own hands, and commit themselves to God again. In return, He will "heal our apostasy and love us freely." Again, God compares Himself to the morning dew that gives life to the flowers and trees of the field each morning. Although exile is on the horizon, "they shall return and dwell" beneath God's shadow in the fruitful land of the promise. Hosea ministers in a time of great political and social degradation and wickedness.

> It is not surprising that Hosea ... pronounced Israel's doom; she was already doomed. The marvel is that he could antici-pate beyond that doom a new and unmerited act of the divine grace, which would bring Israel back from the wilderness ... and restore once more the covenant bond between people and God.[9]

---

prophets creatively make use of a limited number of metaphors for different purposes.

9. Bright, *History*, 273.

This path out of exile and back into the land plants the seeds for the prophets after Hosea to speak of a new exodus and a new covenant, which come to fruition in the New Testament under Christ.

The book ends with a question, "Who is wise? Let him understand these things. Who is discerning? Let him know them" (14:9). This is a formula used often in the wisdom literature (Ecclesiastes, Songs of Solomon, Job, and Proverbs) to hint that this message is not simple but takes patience and contemplation to understand. "Indeed, one way to define a wise person is if he or she is motivated to ponder the mysteries within the book and learn from them."[10] But this is not simply a matter of discernment, but also "the wisdom of a patterned, disciplined response to the ways revealed"[11] by God throughout the book. This final verse is God's plea throughout the book that His people come to know Him with heart, soul, and mind.

Reflection Questions

1. Try to put yourself in Hosea's shoes. What do you imagine he was thinking as God commanded him to do all these things?

2. Do you think Hosea gained a deeper appreciation for God's love through his unfaithful marriage? How so?

3. Chapter 3 talks a lot about God's love. In what ways is God's love different than our own? In what way is it similar? What are some other New

---

10. J. Andrew Dearman, *The Book of Hosea,* NICOT (Grand Rapids: Eerdmans, 2010), 345.

11. Dearman, *Hosea,* 345.

Testament passages that remind you of the love displayed in Hosea 3?

4. In our section on "What manner of man is the prophet," which of the 10 did you see most clearly in Hosea?

5. Is forgiveness hard/difficult for God? How have you battled with forgiveness in your lifetime? How does the story of God's forgiveness help you in your daily walk?

6. Fretheim states, "Thinking of God as judge, remember that the judge behind the bench is the spouse of the accused one in the dock." In what ways did you see this on display throughout Hosea?

Chapter 5

The Book of Micah

Then at last, to keep himself awake, he crawled from the hiding-place and looked out. The land seemed full of creaking and cracking and sly noises, but there was no sound of voice or foot. Far above the Ethel Dúath in the West the night-sky was still dim and pale. There, peeping among the cloud-wrack above a dark tor high up in the mountains, Sam saw a white star twinkle for a while. The beauty of it smote his heart, as he looked up out of the forsaken land, and hope returned to him. For like a shaft, clear and cold, the thought pierced him that in the end the Shadow was only a small and passing thing: there was light and high beauty for ever beyond its reach.[1]

— J.R.R. Tolkien, *The Return of the King*

LONG AGO, there lived a king whose palace sat upon a hill overlooking the city. Just below him lived a simple farmer who

---

1. J.R.R Tolkien, *The Return of the King* (Boston: Houghton Mifflin, 1955), 199.

owned a very fruitful vineyard. Impressed with its productivity, the king visited the farmer and offered a generous price for his land, but the farmer refused the deal. The farmer ironically recites the laws of the land to the king, which forbid him to sell his family property. The king storms off in anger and spends the night sulking in his bed, not because a peasant farmer had to remind the king how to correctly obey God's laws, but because of jealousy and envy. His wife, who also has no knowledge or respect for the law, devises a plan to have the farmer unjustly accused of speaking against their God and king. Being found guilty, he was taken outside the city and stoned to death. They sent word back to the queen, confirming that the plan had been executed.

> As soon as Jezebel heard that Naboth had been stoned and was dead, Jezebel said to Ahab, "Arise, take possession of the vineyard of Naboth the Jezreelite, which he refused to give you for money, for Naboth is not alive, but dead." As soon as he heard that Naboth was dead, "Ahab arose to go down to the vineyard and take possession of it (1 Kings 21:15–16).

The story of Naboth's vineyard epitomizes the current state of Judah's leaders in the eyes of Micah the prophet. "We sense that the Naboth narrative is no one-off incidental transaction. This is rather a window into the systemic practices that pervaded ancient Israel."[2] While the story used in 1 Kings gives a window into the corruption of Ahab, Micah uses this familiar story to rebuke those currently in charge of Judah. Though the prophets accuse Israel and Judah of many different sins, the

---

2. Walter Brueggemann, "What Naboth Teaches Us Today: Part II," https://churchanew.org/brueggemann/what-naboth-teaches-us-today-part-ii#:~:text=From%20my%20initial%20exposition%20of,dispute%20between%20YHWH%20and%20Baal.

most popular accusation is idolatry. Even Isaiah, who is a contemporary of Micah and ministering at the same time, focuses often on the foolishness and evil of idolatry. For Micah, however, the key sin within Israel will be covetousness, which has taken over the hearts of Judah's leaders.

Micah will make two specific allusions to the story of Naboth in an effort to denounce the current leadership. Micah begins his message in chapter 2 with the lamenting cry, "Woe to those who devise wickedness and work evil on their beds!" The word "woe"

> is the cry of lamentation which was customarily heard throughout ancient Israel's clans whenever death struck home. According to Micah's adaptation of this woe, the selfish schemers are actually rotting corpses.[3]

He then goes on to explain his outcry: it is a result of the powerful taking prey of the weak. The second verse of the chapter gives a two-sentence summary of the story of Naboth, which is now used to describe the rulers in Judah. As he brings his message to a close in chapter 6, he again mentions the evil works of the house of Omri. History repeats itself as the covetousness and injustice of King Ahab continue in the lives of Judah's leaders.

* * *

The Downfall of Israel and the Rise of Assyria

The military conquests of Shalmaneser III, king of Assyria,

---

3. Hans Walter Wolff, *Micah the Prophet* (Philadelphia: Fortress Press, 1981), 8.

proved to weaken the nation in numerous ways. They were not equipped for such a fast expansion, so a period of weakness followed. Tiglath-Pileser III would take the throne several years later and rebuild the nation to its most powerful and profitable period. "Within five years of taking power, Tiglath-pileser (Pul) had reestablished Assyria's security against Babylon and Urartu . . . became the first Neo-Assyrian king formally to take the Babylonian throne."[4] After the extremely important Syro-Ephraimite War, Pul killed King Pekah of Israel and put Hoshea on the throne as a puppet king.

In 727, Tiglath-Pileser III died, and hope emerged for the surrounding nations as Shalmaneser V took the throne. Hoshea, seeing this as an opportunity to free Israel from tyranny, withheld tribute and turned to Egypt for help (cf. Isaiah 30:1–7). Unfortunately for him, this was one of Egypt's weakest periods in history. They had been on a downward slide for a while and hit their weakest point with the 22nd and 23rd dynasties (ca. 730–725), which is exactly when Hoshea reached out for an alliance. King Shalmaneser of Assyria responded to the revolt by beginning what would become a three-year siege of the city, culminating in the fall of Samaria in 722. During this time, Sargon II would usurp the throne in Assyria and finish what was started in Samaria. Captives were now being taken away as exiles into Assyria. Although Sargon was a successful ruler, he did lose control of Babylon to Marduk-apla-iddina II (called Merodach-baladan in 2 Kings 20:12 and Isaiah 39:1) but was able to reclaim the city three years later. Samaria then became an Assyrian provincial city, importing their own people and establishing their own rulers in Israel's territory.

While leading a campaign in the West, Sargon met an

---

4. Arnold and Strawn, *World*, 47.

unusual death (perhaps mentioned in Isaiah 14:18–20; cf. Arnold and Strawn, 50), and his son, Sennacherib, took his place. Sennacherib moved the capital city to Nineveh and is most known for his devastating excursion into Judean territory. Upon his rise to the throne, Judah and the surrounding nations sought a chance for rebellion. In 701 BCE, Sennacherib stormed through the Levant and pillaged 46 cities (possibly including Moresheth, the home of Micah). His conquest ended with Jerusalem, which was miraculously saved from destruction (Isaiah 36–39). He was then killed by his brothers soon after his return to Assyria.

* * *

This is the world in which the prophet Micah emerges. It is for this reason that the LORD is coming out of His place and visiting the nation with a heavy hand (1:3). He first addresses Samaria, the capital of Israel. Because of their transgression, destruction will befall the city. What was once a prosperous and flowing metropolis will soon become "a heap in an open country." The city will be uprooted from its foundation and cast into the valley. As much as Judah wants to see themselves as separated from their wayward northern brother, the sin of Israel has spread like a sickness to the gates of Jerusalem (1:9). Just as Judah is not immune to the sin of Israel, so they are not immune to the foreign oppression that is coming. In the years following Israel's destruction and exile, Sennacherib of Assyria launched a campaign into Judah territory, destroying several small towns on his way to destroy the capital city. This move is announced by a series of word plays from Micah starting in verse 10 and running through the end of the first chapter.[5] The

---

5. Wolff, *Prophets*, 41.

wordplay Micah uses would be like saying, "You think you are fine now, but you are about to be *fine* (Italian for 'end' or 'finished')." He does this, not to be clever or artistic, but to make his message unforgettable and show that things are going to be very different than they seem if they continue walking this path.

In the last panel of the 1962 *Amazing Fantasy* #15 comic book, Stan Lee records the thoughts of his main character at the end of the story, saying, "and a lean, silent figure slowly fades in the gathering darkness, aware at last that in this world, with great power there must also come—great responsibility!" That famous character is Spider-Man, and those famous words are later attributed in the movies to Uncle Ben, but they have a much longer history. During the chaotic Napoleonic Wars, British parliament member William Lamb proclaimed in a heated debate that "the possession of great power necessarily implies great responsibility." There are several other examples of similar thoughts and phrases throughout history, all giving evidence to the seemingly universal idea that those in power have a responsibility to those under their control. This is the reason for God's anger in the book of Micah. At the beginning of chapter 2, those who "devise evil in their beds" wake up the following morning and perform it without any issue. The ease of their wickedness comes from the fact that "it is in the power of their hands" to perform it. Instead of those in charge looking upon their kingdom and seeing responsibility, they see frailty and take advantage of it.

Chapter 2 begins by reversing the fortunes of the nation as the LORD "devises disaster" against His own people (2:1–5). Everything their greed has taken will soon be given to their enemy. Verse 6 records the people's response as they quickly try to silence Micah's preaching. In their reply, they argue, "We are not to blame! You are wrong to think that shame will overtake us … God's patience with us has *not* been exhausted.

These ominous developments of which you speak are *not* God's doing! God is not out to get us!"[6] Micah responds with some rhetorical questions saying that God does protect His own people, "but lately my people have risen up as an enemy" (2:8). As a result, Israel will now be treated as enemies for abusing the poor and needy among them—those of whom they had a responsibility to protect. Unfortunately, the nation has become so corrupt and calloused that the only person they would accept as a true preacher is a drunken liar (2:11), so Micah's message is rejected. The chapter ends with a glimmer of hope as God promises to gather the remnant of Israel and lead them out of exile as their one true king and shepherd His people, foreshadowing the work of Christ.

Chapter 3 returns to the indictment upon Judah's leaders as he opens with the piercing command, "Listen!" He asks rhetorically, again, "Is it not for you to know justice" as leaders of the nation? The idea is not that they know intellectually what is right and wrong, but that they should be the ones who exemplify it the most. This is the same word used throughout the book of Hosea. Their actions should be the closest example of living life according to the law. Instead, they are the exact opposite of what they were called to be. In graphic detail, he describes the effects of their action upon the people. It is possible that the flaying of skin and the tearing of flesh were Assyrian torture tactics. If that is the case, the leaders of Israel are pictured as Assyrians torturing and killing their own people. He then turns to the prophets who deliver good predictions when given the right price, but announce judgment when not compensated as they wish. Both actions lead to God turning away from His people. They will cry to God, but He

---

6. Terence Fretheim, *Reading Hosea-Micah* (Macon, GA: Smyth & Helwys, 2013), 200.

will not answer. They will seek a word from God, but He will remain silent. Who is going to be brave enough or wise enough to stand up to these rebellious people?

Micah then announces his credentials (3:8). God has given him this divine mission and the power to announce the truth to these wicked nations that are blinded by sin. What is the essence of that message? It is you, the leaders of God's people, who have taken God's presence for granted and taken divine chosenness to mean divine partiality. They have treated God's presence with contempt and, as a result, have brought upon their own destruction.

Chapters 4 and 5 break away from the message of doom and gloom and provide strong messages of hope and salvation. It begins with a vision of life in God's kingdom upon an exalted mountain that serves as a beacon to the nations. These first few verses in chapter 4 are extremely similar to Isaiah 2:2–5, leading many to question how they are related. Isaiah and Micah were contemporaries, but there is no solid evidence that they knew each other. There have been many theories thrown out, but no definitive answer has been given. However, it is not surprising that this image would resonate in their day. Perhaps God wanted to reinforce that the evil and corruption that pervades the land will not have the final say. Yes, God's judgment is coming, but there will also come a day when all who come to God's holy mountain will learn and know the ways of God (contrasted to the leaders who "don't know justice"), and each will find rest in his own fruitful vineyard (contrasted to life under current leadership where one finds "no place of rest" 2:10).

The reader is brought back to the present in the middle of chapter 4 and reminded that, like a woman in labor, pain must come before life (a very common image used throughout the pre-exilic prophets). This reflects a common theme in the book where judgment and salvation are more closely tied than we would like.

> This movement from judgement to salvation, from suffering to redemption, is a basic rhythm in Micah and in prophetic thought more generally. Judgement is believed to be inevitable for a sinful people (see 1:13); it is only *through* judgement (and the suffering that it brings) that salvation can become a reality.[7]

This section of Micah and its corresponding passage in Isaiah 2 are often highlighted as pacifist passages with the main idea being the cessation of war between nations, but that seems to give an inconsistent picture when paired with Micah 4:12–13 where Zion (God's people) will rise up to destroy the nations. It is important to note that the idea of peace (*shalom* in Hebrew) has an extremely wide meaning in the Bible. Peace in terms of the absence of war is only a small part of a much larger picture. At its core, peace means to be whole or complete and is used in relationships to describe the close connection between two parties. The shalom, or peace, that Israel will soon experience on the other side of captivity will center around God's right relationship with His people. The cessation of war may be a by-product of that in the world to come, but the key idea is God's presence.[8] This is the prominent reason for hope in Chapter 5. In contrast to the evil, manipulative rulers of Micah's day, there shall come forth "a ruler in Israel, whose coming forth is from of old, from ancient days … he shall stand

---

7. Fretheim, *Reading*, 209.

8. Chris van Der Walt, "Peace is not the Absence of War but the Presence of a Relationship Founded by God—שלום (*shalom*) in Isaiah and Micah," *In die Skrifling* 55 (2021): 1–8.

and shepherd his flock in the strength of the LORD ... and he shall be their peace" (5:1–6).

* * *

A Ruler from Bethlehem

"Micah consciously predicted that the tiny city of Bethlehem would produce an Israelite king "whose goings out are from aforetime, from ancient times [or, 'from days of eternity'] ... this final clause suggests a king who is more than a mere human."[9] This verse is later quoted in Matthew 2 announcing the birth of Christ. Matthew adds the phrase "by no means" before "insignificant" to show that "Bethlehem was insignificant by world standards, but once it was graced with the birth of the Messiah, it was no longer insignificant."[10] Matthew also alludes to 2 Samuel 5:2 saying this ruler "will shepherd my people." This sets up a clear distinction between the current leaders of Micah's day and one who would come as a true leader of God's people. "And he shall be their peace" (Micah 5:5).

* * *

The final section of chapter 5 brings up the image of the "remnant of Jacob" and the nation's future. Thinking of Israel in exile, I would often picture "the remnant" as a protected group; those who were shielded from the pains of exile. I would naively imagine a group walking through exile with a bubble around them, just waiting for God to pick them up and put them back in the land. But the way that the word "remnant" is

---

9. Carson and Beale, *Commentary*, 6.
10. Carson and Beale, *Commentary*, 6

used in the prophets is more like leftovers or remainders. The same word is used for what is left over after a tree gets cut to the ground (cf. the imagery of a shoot from the stump in Isaiah). Wolff describes the remnant of Jacob as "the community of those who have been liberated from the prison into which God's judgement had put them."[11] Perhaps you had a better understanding of the remnant than I did, but it is still worth mentioning that this image of a remnant is not a group protected from judgment, but one who is delivered out of it by a gracious God. It will be this battered group of people who will soon be formed into a mighty nation with the LORD as their new king (5:6–7). "Its wounds are actually its strength. That fact the lame and the halt should grasp firmly."[12]

The end of the book returns to the topic of judgment, but shows that this judgment does not come flippantly. Chapter 6 opens with a plea from God to His people. The LORD lays His heart on the table, soliciting a response from Judah. He rhetorically asks, "How have I wearied you?" He then follows with a list of key moments in Israel's history where God has intervened to save them: delivery from slavery in Egypt, the story of Balaam intervening to stop Balak's curse on Israel, and two key locations in Israel's crossing of the Jordan into the promised land. "Look at what I have done for you!" God declares. And what does the LORD seek from you? To do what is right/just, to be devoted to the covenant (Hebrew: *hesed*), and walk humbly with your God (6:8). Yet, there is no response. "'Answer Me!' calls the voice of God. But who hears the call? "The voice of the LORD cries to the city" (6:9), but the city is complacent."[13]

---

11. Wolff, *Micah*, 89.
12. Wolff, *Micah*, 89. Cf. 2 Corinthians 12:8–10.
13. Heschel, *Prophets*, 127.

Instead of following the way of God, they have "kept the statutes of Omri, and all the works of the house of Ahab; and you have walked in their counsels" (6:16). As a result, destruction will come for Judah as well as Israel. Both cities will be made a desolation. Micah stands alone as the people reject his passionate plea from God. Remarkably, despite the scorn and rejection, Micah is able to look ahead to a time of salvation.

> Among the great insights Micah has bequeathed to us is how to accept and to bear the anger of God. The strength of acceptance comes from the awareness that we have sinned against Him and from the certainty that anger does not mean God's abandonment of man forever. His anger passes, His faithfulness goes on forever. There is compassion in His anger; when we fall, we rise. Darkness is not dismal.[14]

Micah (whose name means "who is like Yahweh") ends the book in a very fitting manner, asking, "Who is a God like you?" A God who has compassion for a people who continually reject Him. The final section of the book (7:18–20) beautifully anticipates the work of Christ on the cross.

> Who is a God like you, pardoning iniquity and passing over transgression for the remnant of His inheritance? He does not retain His anger forever, because He delights in steadfast love (hesed). He will again have compassion on us; he will tread our iniquities underfoot. You will cast all our sins into the depths of the sea (Micah 7:18–19).

---

14. Heschel, Prophets, 128. Cf. Micah 7:7–10.

Reflection Questions

1. Have you ever been in a position of power? How did you use that position responsibly? How can we use positions of power/influence for evangelism?
2. Wolff points out three sins found in the leaders that become the root cause of all the injustice found in the city: coveting what belongs to others, perverting justice, and hypocritical religiosity.[15] Where do you see those on display throughout Israel and Judah's history? In the world today?
3. In our section on "What manner of man is the prophet," which of the 10 did you see most clearly in Micah?
4. Micah says that God has told us what is *good*. What is *good* according to God? What does the world tell us is good? How do we fall prey to the world's definition of good rather than God's?
5. How is God present with His people today? What does God's presence mean for us? What does it require from us?
6. Read Micah 7:18–20. How is the life of Christ reflected in this passage?
7. Micah reminds the remnant that they, too, will have to endure hardship, but to wait for the coming salvation. What does that mean for God's people today? How can/should we view and endure hardship? (Read 2 Corinthians 12:1–10).

---

15. Wolff, *Micah*, 8.

Chapter 6

The Book of Isaiah

*"W*ILL *you come with me to the mountains? It will hurt at first, until your feet are hardened. Reality is harsh to the feet of shadows. But will you come?" "Well, that is a plan. I am perfectly ready to consider it. Of course I should require some assurances ... I should want a guarantee that you are taking me to a place where I shall find a wider sphere of usefulness—and scope for the talents that God has given me." ... "I can promise you none of these things. No sphere of usefulness: you are not needed there at all. No scope for your talents: only forgiveness for having perverted them. No atmosphere of inquiry, for I will bring you to the land not of questions but of answers, and you shall see the face of God."* [1]

— C. S. Lewis, *The Great Divorce*

The book of Isaiah is a beautifully complex anthology that

---

1. C. S. Lewis, *The Great Divorce*, in *The C.S. Lewis Signature Classics* (New York: Harper Collins, 2017), 486–7.

moves like a symphony through various themes, images, and even genres throughout the book. This persistent shift in tone and style enhances the book's beauty and magnificence, though it also introduces a level of difficulty for the reader. Many try to alleviate the difficulty by forming an outline of the book, but this can further complicate things if not done carefully. Still, a division of the book is helpful, so we will follow an outline of history rather than composition. In a very loose way, the beginning of the book, through chapter 35, focuses on the current crisis and Assyrian dominion, chapters 40–66 are written from a future perspective after the Babylonian captivity, and chapters 36–39 are a historical narrative that transitions between the two sections. As we have seen already, the message of the prophets cannot be separated from the political climate of their day. The prophet speaks to a specific people in a specific historical situation. To better understand the message, we must understand the world around him. This will become immensely important for the book of Isaiah, as the historical and political settings have a strong influence on the prophet's message.

Seeing the disastrous effects of Israel's sin and corruption following the reign of Jeroboam II, it would be tempting for Judah to think of itself as morally and politically superior to their wayward brother. It is at this point, in the days of Uzziah, that Isaiah is sent to proclaim a devastating message to the people of Judah, "Ah, sinful nation, a people laden with iniquity, offspring of evildoers ... If the LORD of hosts had not left us a few survivors, we should have been like Sodom, and become like Gomorrah" (1:4, 9). The whole nation "from the sole of the foot even to the head" (1:6) is sick and in need of repentance. The allusion to the two wicked cities is no accident. Poignancy becomes a necessity for a people oblivious to sin.

Until repentance becomes a reality, the abundance of sacrifices, the core of Israelite worship, becomes fruitless and vain (1:10–15). Imagine being a priest at this time, every day being covered in the blood of bulls and goats, only to be told that all your efforts are useless. Or, as an owner of livestock, having to present your best animals before the altar, only to be told all your sacrifices are worthless. Isaiah uses this heavy language to show that, because worship is a matter of the heart, it cannot be separated from our daily lives. They cannot live in sin and expect to walk into the temple thinking all is well. "When you spread out your hands, I will hide my eyes from you; even though you make many prayers, I will not listen; your hands are full of blood" (1:15). Jesus teaches something similar in the Sermon on the Mount, where He talks about anger within the heart while at the altar (Matthew 5:21–26).

We are quickly introduced to Isaiah's sporadic writing style in verse 18 as a flash of hope emerges from the rhetoric of judgment. "Though your sins are like scarlet, they shall be as white as snow" (1:18). An ultimatum is then laid before them, which will echo throughout Isaiah's message. If they obey and repent, then goodness will follow, but if they refuse and turn away, then they will be devoured by the sword (1:19–20). So begins Isaiah's heartfelt plea to turn the hearts of his people back to their God.

Isaiah will often use similar imagery to Hosea when revealing the moral corruption of the nation (1:21–24). He reveals how foreign religion and idolatry have swept through the nation, leading the hearts of the people astray (2:6–9). Against this corruption, the anger of the LORD will be kindled, but not forever. Isaiah often uses contrasting images to distinguish Israel's current situation from the promises to come. Though the nation is currently full of sin (1:21), soon it will be restored to its beginnings as a faithful city (1:26). Though foreign religion plagues the nation now; in the latter days, the mountain of the LORD will rise, and all nations will flow to it as they come to know God's ways (2:2–3).

Chapter 3 provides a more tangible picture of the state of the nation and what lies ahead for those currently dwelling in Judah. The closing verses (3:24–4:1) vividly depict the warriors of their city falling by the sword, leaving the survivors to begin their journey as prisoners into captivity—a nightmare that will soon be a reality in just a few generations. Yet, there is hope. Amid the destruction, a branch will emerge from the drought. Life will spring out of death. This is the great paradox of the prophetic message; it is only in death that they will truly be able to experience life. "In that day the branch of the LORD shall be beautiful and glorious, and the fruit of the land shall be the pride and honor of the survivors of Israel" (4:2). Here Isaiah the botanist establishes himself as he will often use plant and vegetation imagery to show the death of the nation (either in terms of desert/wilderness language, or a field that has grown thorns and thistles that choke out the good fruit) and the future hope that sprouts in an unlikely area (ch. 4).

Several of Isaiah's themes are combined in a clever parable in chapter 5.[2] He tells the story of a gardener who did everything he could to provide the perfect habitat for his vineyard. He patiently waited for them to yield their fruit, but despite his best efforts, the produce proved to be useless. Stunned by the result, the gardener asks, "What more could I have done for my vineyard?" An explanation of the parable is provided in verse 7, identifying God as the gardener, and Israel and Judah as the vine. With brilliant use of wordplay, Isaiah shows how God planted Israel and Judah in a fruitful land and provided every-

---

2. This parable is alluded to by Jesus in his parable of the tenets, Matthew 21:33–46.

thing for them in hopes that they would produce justice and righteousness, yet all He found was bloodshed and outcry (the Hebrew words for justice (*mishpat*) and bloodshed (*mispach*) sound alike, and the words righteousness (*tsedeqah*) and outcry (*tse'aqah*) sound alike). The people have turned away from what they were called to be, so exile awaits them (5:13).

Chapter 6 breaks the trail of thought a bit and records a vision seen by Isaiah, which occurs at a crucial time in Israel's history. Most commentators are puzzled by the placement of this vision since prophets usually receive their message and mission at the beginning of the book, not years after their ministry has already begun. The most important part of this section, however, is not Isaiah's call to ministry, but the message he is told to deliver. After encountering the LORD upon His throne surrounded by seraphim, Isaiah himself is brought into the picture and told to proclaim a message that will harden the hearts of the people (6:9–10). This message will become a key text in the New Testament, where it is quoted six different times while making an appearance in all four gospels. Each time it is used as a reference to God's people rejecting His word and salvation through Christ. This same rejection will be displayed by Judah and King Ahaz in the very next chapter of Isaiah.

* * *

The Syro-Ephraimite War

King Ahaz inherited the throne from his father, Uzziah, and immediately walked into one of the most difficult political situations in Judah's history. Irate and exasperated with Assyrian oppression, King Rezin of Damascus and King Pekah of Israel joined forces with some other smaller nations in a rebellion against Assyria. After a failed attempt to get Ahaz to join the coalition, they began to march on Jerusalem in hopes that they might overtake the city and replace Ahaz with a puppet king who was sympathetic to their cause (7:6; a move that would have ended the Davidic line). At the same time, the Edomites were attacking from the south along with the Philistines from the coast. In a very turbulent time, Isaiah pleads with Ahaz to remain patient, trust in God, and not allow "these smoldering stumps" (7:4) to force him into making a grave mistake.

Ahaz, seeing no other option for survival, turns to the world powerhouse at the time for protection (2 Kings 16:7). Ahaz, incapable of the faith Isaiah calls him to, sends tribute to Tiglath-Pileser III, effectively pitting themselves against Israel. Assyria squashed the rebellion, killed both Rezin and Pekah, and then placed Hoshea on the throne as a puppet king, which essentially ended the nation of Israel. Hosea gained the throne by pledging support to Assyria, but upon the death of Tiglath Pileser III, he tried to rebel against them by seeking support from a very weak Egyptian empire. Egypt, itself in a position of need, made for a poor alliance, which would lead to the downfall of Samaria.

* * *

Chapter 7 takes place at the very beginning of the Syro-Ephraimite War. The first several verses poetically recount the political situation that is occurring and the fear it sends throughout Judah. Isaiah is sent to plead for Ahaz not to act in fear and allow the rising war to pass over. Instead, the king refuses the counsel of the prophet—the man sent by God. Even though Ahaz tries desperately to keep God out of the situation, the LORD forces Himself into the story anyway. God sends a sign to the reluctant king, saying, "Behold, the *young woman* shall conceive and bear a son and shall call his name Immanuel" (7:14). There is a big debate over the exact meaning and even translation of this verse. The ESV translates "young woman" as "virgin" based on an old Greek translation called the Septuagint. The matter is too dense to cover in full detail, but some important aspects need to be mentioned to help understand the passage.

The debate largely centers on the identity of the son in the passage—is this a prophecy about the future Messiah, or is it a prophecy to be fulfilled in Isaiah's day? Reading Isaiah alone and in context favors the second option, which says this prophecy will be fulfilled in the days of Ahaz. This is strengthened by the fact that the term "young woman" in Hebrew (almah) doesn't necessarily mean virgin, but a woman of marriageable age. Several centuries later, when the text was copied into Greek, the writer used the word parthenos, which specifically means virgin. This was the version quoted in the gospel of Matthew when recording the coming of Christ (Matthew 1:23). Following Carson and Beale, it is best to see this episode as an example of double fulfillment where a prophecy has a specific meaning in its current context and is also used to refer to something else in the future.[3] Isaiah is using this sign to show just how quickly this alliance between King Rezin and King Pekah will be broken; before the boy born to the young woman knows how to distinguish between evil and good, the situation will be deserted (7:14–16). This is a sign that the word of the LORD is true despite the rejection by His people. Christ is a sign of the same. In both Isaiah's day and in the New Testament, the word of the LORD will remain true, despite the people's unbelief (cf. 8:5–10).

---

3. Carson and Beale, Commentary, 4–5.

* * *

Following this sign will be a period of darkness and vanity that hasn't been seen since the division of the kingdom (7:17). But in a later time, "the people who walked in darkness will see a great light" (9:2). In chapters 8 and 9 you get a fuller sense of the double fulfillment of Isaiah's prophecy a chapter ago. Immanuel is mentioned again, along with Isaiah's claim that God sent him children as signs to Israel (8:18–showing that Isaiah is speaking of his current day, but that the prophecy takes on a different meaning later in the New Testament). Isaiah quickly transitions to a time of hope and peace that will be ushered in through the birth of another child (9:6–7). This child will take the throne of David and reign as no king has ever reigned before (Luke 1:32–33, Revelation 19:16).

* * *

Jesus and The Land of Zebulun and Naphtali (Isaiah 9; Matthew 4:19; Luke 1:67–79, 2:29–32)

While Isaiah 8 warns of the destruction and darkness that is coming for Judah, the ninth chapter looks past the darkness to a time of hope and comfort.

> In the former time he brought into contempt the land of Zebulun and the land of Naphtali, but in the latter time he has made glorious the way of the sea, the land beyond the Jordan, Galilee of the nations. The people who walked in darkness have seen a great light; those who dwelt in a land of deep darkness, on them has light shone (Isaiah 9:1–2).

This passage is quoted in Matthew 4:12–17 as Jesus begins

his preaching ministry "to fulfill what Isaiah had spoken." The outer rim of the Israelite kingdom (Zebulun and Naphtali) would be the first ones to experience the devastating conquest of Tiglath-Pileser III that swept through the Israelite nation. In the time of Jesus, they will be the first ones to experience the light of hope and salvation through Christ. Though the people have returned from exile, they still find themselves lost in the darkness of sin and death (Luke 1:79). Christ comes as the saving hope (Matthew 4:19), not only for Israel but for all the nations of the earth (Luke 2:30–32).

* * *

Though the future promises hope, the current day remains dark and gloomy for God's people. The Assyrians will eventually come and overtake the Israelite nation and carry them into exile. Although the nation has been made numerous "like the sand of the sea," only a remnant will remain. But Assyria, the mighty nation, will also face the judgment of God (10:12–25). Once the yoke of Assyrian oppression is lifted, Israel will be able to commit themselves wholly to their God. On that day, though Israel is reduced to a stump, a shoot shall emerge from the line of Jesse, upon whom the spirit of the LORD will descend—one who fears the LORD, judges with righteousness, and is dressed in faithfulness. On that day, there will be a second Exodus of God's people along with the nations (11:11, 15–16). Salvation is on the horizon.

The following sections (chs. 13–23) are largely composed of oracles against the nations surrounding Judah and Israel. The Babylonians take center stage in chapter 14 as Isaiah is told to take up a "taunt" against the king of Babylon. Isaiah will "bring to life the inner truth of the king,"[4] revealing his weakness and frailty. In this "taunt," there is a section that is often interpreted as the origin story of Satan. In his address to the king, Isaiah says, "How you are fallen from heaven, O Day Star, son of Dawn! How you are cut down from the ground, you who laid the nations low!" Jerome, in his Latin translation of the Old Testament, translated "day star" as "lucifer," which provided links to passages in Revelation (Revelation 12:19) and in the words of Jesus (Luke 10:18) that the early church fathers connected with Satan. While links certainly can be made, it seems clear that Isaiah is referring to the pride and coming downfall of the king of Babylon. Could later writers refer back to these words when describing the fall of Satan? Yes. But in the current context, this passage provides a sharp warning to the rising nation of Babylon and her king. Though his glory seems to shine like the brightest star in the sky, he will soon be brought to the depths of Sheol and made a mockery among the nations.

The oracles of judgment take a break toward the end of chapter 19, where there is a picture of future hope, not only for Israel but for Assyria and Egypt as well. There will be a day coming when Israel, along with her enemies and oppressors, will come together to worship the one true God. This is the culmination of a lesson that began with Jonah and has worked its way through the prophets—that this world belongs to God, and He desires for all His creation to be joined to Himself. This contains a couple of lessons that God's people must learn. First, they must realize that it is "neither Pekah, Rezin, or Tiglath Pileser III who govern history, the world is in the hands

---

4. Don Shackleford, *Isaiah*, Truth for Today Commentary (Searcy, AR: Resource Publications, 2005), 183.

of God."[5] Second, God's plans have always been and will always be for all people. Isaiah doesn't appeal to Assyria and Egypt by accident. Like the book of Jonah, the message is that "they, even they, are a part of God's plans."

Chapters 24–27 make up a unit that breaks away from the oracles of judgment on specific nations and focuses on the earth as a whole. All the land is guilty and defiled. As a result, the land will come to waste and be destroyed. Images of barrenness and desolation fill the early pages of the section, but amid the deserted land rises the Mountain of the LORD, where the people eat and drink in peace and where death and destruction are swallowed up forever. The land of Judah will be a place of peace, protection, and refuge. It will be the LORD's vineyard (27:2 cf. ch. 5), which will produce enough fruit to fill the earth.

* * *

A Sign against Egypt and Cush (Isaiah 20)

Shortly after the fall of Samaria and the exile of the northern kingdom (722 BCE), Ethiopian king Piankhi took over Upper Egypt and established a powerful 24th dynasty. "In view of these signs of resurgence, Assyrian vassals in Palestine might dare once more to look to Egypt for help."[6] One of those cities was Ashdod, a Philistine town that usurped its ruler and sought to overthrow their Assyrian overlord. Other surrounding cities joined in for a chance to take down the world power, but Sargon marched over to stomp out the rebellion, and the usurping Ashdod king fled to Egypt for refuge. The new

---

5. Heschel, *Prophets*, 82.
6. Bright, *History*, 281.

Egyptian king then handed him over to the Assyrians, who took him as a prisoner. This is the setting of Isaiah's plea in chapter 20 and why he walks around naked and barefoot—to show how these rising kings will end up after their rebellion against Assyria.

* * *

In the current day, all of God's people have rebelled and turned away from Him. Like a stubborn child, they are unwilling to lend an ear to God's instructions. They even go to the prophets and seers (30:8–11) and ask to soften the message that is given to them. They say, "Do not prophesy to us what is right; speak to us smooth things, prophesy illusions, leave the way, turn aside from the path, let us hear no more about the Holy One of Israel" (30:10–11). Christian writer Beth Moore once said, "When our story is told a century from now ... history will not only fault the [preachers] for not confronting us with the truth, but the congregations who forbade them to." It is important that we are confronted with the sin in and around us, or we too will blind and deafen ourselves to destruction. How we handle the word of God is extremely important. For those who hear the word, we must learn to accept both its edification and its discipline. For those who proclaim the message, we need to remember the very words of Isaiah, "I am lost, for I am a man of unclean lips, and I dwell in the midst of a people of unclean lips" (6:5). Once we acknowledge, confess, and repent; we can have hope in a God who "waits to be gracious" to us (30:18).

* * *

King Hezekiah and Sennacherib (chs. 36–39)

Upon the death of Sargon, his son Sennacherib would take the throne. Like most transitions of power, this provided a flash of hope for King Hezekiah, who saw a chance for rebellion and independence. Judah was not the only nation thinking along these lines, as many nations were eager to free their people from the heavy yoke of Assyrian domination. Among these nations would be the kingdom of Babylon, just south of Assyria, which would prove to be a constant thorn in the side of Sennacherib.

Shortly after Sennacherib's rise to the throne, he was met with a rebellion from the Babylonian King Marduk-apal-idinna (Merodach-Baladan in the Bible). Babylon sent envoys west to conjure a rebellion (ch. 39), enlisting both Judah and Egypt. Another coalition was also forming, with Tyre summoning Moab, Edom, and Ammon. Hezekiah was met with both options, but Isaiah urged him not to join (30:1–5, 31:1–3). It was at this time that Hezekiah, seeing war on the horizon, began to build his famous Siloam tunnel that would bring water from Gihon underneath Jerusalem to a pool in the city in the event that an enemy would besiege Jerusalem.

After muzzling the Babylonian rebellion, Sennacherib turned toward the rebellions in the west, looking to reassert Assyrian rule. He quickly dismantled the hopeful coalitions, capturing and destroying forty-six cities and fortresses of Judah. Only Jerusalem and the city of Lachish remained standing. Hezekiah tried to make up for his actions by sending tribute to Sennacherib, but the Assyrian king refused to ignore the insurrection and destroyed the city of Lachish. He then turned his attention toward Jerusalem with the full intent to kill

Hezekiah. After surrounding the city and sending threatening messages to the people (Isaiah 36–37; 2 Kings 18–19), the LORD sent an angel through the Assyrian military camp, killing 185,000 men. Sennacherib returned to Nineveh and lived out the rest of his days there until he was assassinated by his two sons.

The exact timing of all these events is subject to debate. One option is to take the chronology of chapters 36–39 at face value. Two problems arise, however, as 38:6 makes it seem as if the siege of Assyria has yet to happen or that the sickness occurred during the siege of Jerusalem. Also, other extra-biblical documents place Merodach-Baladan's reign (721–703 BCE) to a time before the siege of Jerusalem (701 BCE). To solve these issues, some claim that chapters 36–39 are not in chronological order. It is very possible that the sickness and recovery of Hezekiah (ch. 38) and the envoys of Babylon (ch. 39) occurred before or during the invasion of Assyria. The sequence of events becomes more important for literary purposes than chronology. By placing Hezekiah's failure at the end of the section, the author is "pointing ahead to the coming defeat by Babylon."[7] This solution isn't without its own difficulties, as you must explain why both 2 Kings and 2 Chronicles record the same order of events. Another option is that there are multiple uprisings from Babylon that Sennacherib must draw back and quench, but that lack the historical evidence needed to gain traction. It is easy to get lost in all the intricacies of the issue, but it is helpful to note that the historicity of these events is not in question, just the timing. The core of these chapters does not lie in chronology but in the rise of Babylon as a major power and Hezekiah's weaknesses as a leader.

---

7. John N. Oswalt, *Isaiah*, NIV Application Commentary (Grand Rapids: Zondervan, 2003), 399.

Hezekiah will be a mirror of Jerusalem as a whole in these chapters; on the brink of death, both are delivered by God.

* * *

The arrival of chapter 36 transitions into a small section in the middle of Isaiah's message that provides a historical bridge between the two major sections of the book. Grogan (writing about chapter 39 specifically, but it applies to the entire section) says, "This brief chapter is of great importance because it seems in the overall plan of the book to set the scene for the chapters that follow."[8] While the exact chronology of these chapters can be difficult to determine, it is clear that God's people are again faced with the challenge of trusting God in the midst of political uncertainty. Like a broken record, they fail to exhibit any trust in their God and rely instead on the nations around them. Ironically, the nation of Babylon that they decide to put their trust in will be the same nation that will bring about the destruction and exile of Judah.

Throughout these chapters, it is important to note the difficult position in which Hezekiah was placed. In stories like these, it is easy to highlight the lack of faith within the characters, but perhaps we should also notice just how difficult true faith can be amid uncertainty. The retelling of this story in 2 Chronicles 32:31 calls this a time of testing for Hezekiah to know "all that was in his heart." This is not a rarity. Over and over again throughout the biblical story, we see God testing the hearts of the people. These stories often produce more examples to repudiate than to emulate. But why do these stories flood the pages? Why are we constantly reminded of the fail-

---

8. Geoffrey W. Grogan, *Isaiah*, EBC 6 (Grand Rapids: Zondervan, 1986), 239.

ures of the people? Perhaps it is because these stories are meant
to be read with a mirror, rather than a microscope. Instead of
reading these stories and jumping to criticism, what if we read
these stories with a reflective mind and asked ourselves, "If
God were to peer into my heart right now, what would He
see?"

The Rabshakeh (title of a high-ranking Assyrian military
officer) delivers this message to Judah: "Look at your pitiful
situation. Do you think your God is powerful enough to deliver
you? Do not be fooled. Instead, give your allegiance to Assyria
and her king, and we will be your peace. Surrender, come to
Assyria, and you will receive all the desires of your heart." He
uses the familiar tactic of fear and uncertainty to draw the
hearts of the people away from their God. After trying to instill
fear, he takes the common image of peace and security ("each
man shall sit under his own vine and fig tree"—Micah 4:4, 1
Kings 4:25, Zechariah 3:10) found throughout scripture and
manipulates them. These, he claims, can only be inherited
through the power and wealth of Assyria, not by Israel's God.
Against this message are the tender words of Christ, "Come to
me all who are heavy laden, and I will give you rest."

With the opening of chapter 40, we transition into the final
historical section of the book. This section has sparked a lot of
controversy in recent history regarding the composition of the
book. It has become commonplace in scholarship to view Isaiah
as a product of more than one author. This theory was first
proposed in 1775 by J.C. Döderlein because of the constant
shift in tone and perspective within the book, and primarily
due to the mention of Cyrus of Persia (the Persian empire
would not gain ground until several years after the Babylonian
captivity. Cyrus is the king who would release Israel from
captivity, allowing them to return to their land). The denial of
predictive prophecy, along with several other factors, led him to

conclude that chapters 1–39 were written by Isaiah, but chapters 40–66 were written later by an anonymous author in Babylonian captivity (the title of this mystery author is commonly called "deutero-Isaiah"). Since Döderlein's original hypothesis, there have been several other theories proposing three or even four different authors within the book.

Theories will abound concerning the authorship of Isaiah, but there remains very solid ground to reject them. As Chisholm mentions, just because there is a shift in focus and perspective to captivity, it doesn't automatically follow that there are multiple authors writing before and after exile. Instead, "Isaiah 40–66 can be compared to a grandfather writing a note for his granddaughter with the opening, "To be read on your wedding day." He may speak/write as if he is in the future, though it hasn't happened yet."[9] Isaiah looks past the current Assyrian threat to the deliverance God would bring His people—a people who will soon find themselves in Babylonian captivity. Therefore, it seems best to treat the whole book as authored by Isaiah before the fall of Judah. Still, the book often switches rapidly between themes and subjects, so we will look at the remainder of the book by grouping together common themes instead of taking each chapter seriatim.

Highway out of Captivity (40:1–5, 42:10–17, 43:16–21, 45:2, 48:20–21, 49:8–9, 57:14–15, 61:1–4). In language that at times resembles and even calls back to the Exodus, God announces His plan to bring the people out of their captivity and back into the land of promise. Just like the passage through the Sea, a path will be made out of captivity and back into the land. The mountains will be made low and the valleys raised high, providing safe and easy passage out of their new slavery. This theme is used in the gospel of John, referring to the work

---

9.   Chisholm, *Handbook*, 14.

of John the Baptist, who proclaims, "I am the voice of one calling in the wilderness, make straight the way of the Lord." John announces that salvation is coming in and through Jesus.

God's Faithfulness/Salvation (40:6–8, 9–11, 29–31; 41:1–20; 42:10–17; 43:1–28; 42:21–28; 45:14–25; 48:17–22; 49:8–26; 50:7–11; 51:7–16; 52:1–12; 54:9–10; 57:14–21; 58:1–14; 61:1–11; 63:7–14; 66:12–14). Connected to the previous theme is the promise and reminder of God's faithfulness and His plan to save Israel. From the very beginning, the relationship between God and Israel has been a covenant, a union, and a partnership between two parties. Even though Israel failed to uphold their side of the covenant, God never fails. Although the people are like grass, the word of the LORD remains forever. A common Hebrew word that is tied to this concept is *hesed*, which is translated often as steadfast love, loving faithfulness, love, loving-kindness, or something similar. Really, there is no perfect English equivalent, but the idea is something we all understand: loyalty to a promise. Why is there a highway out of captivity? Why is God committed to extending salvation to His people? Why is God still bothering to deal with Israel when they betray Him time and time again? Because the *hesed* of the LORD never ceases, His mercies never come to an end; they are new every morning (Lamentations 3:22–23).

Mountain of the LORD/High Mountain (40:9; 56:1–8; 57:12–21; 65:11, 17–25). As Isaiah continues to bounce back and forth between present and future, the image of God united with His people on a Holy Mountain dominates the future to come for those who follow God. Mount Zion, as it is referred to elsewhere, "became *the* mountain of God for Israel, the mountain that will eventually be exalted over all the earth, transformed into Eden ... dwelling with God."[10] This mountain

---

10. L. Michael Morales, *Who Shall Ascend the Mountain of the Lord?: A*

becomes the key image in the future hope for Israel. "The prophets threaten Israel with death in the form of exile from God's Presence in Zion; and they promise Israel life afterward in the form of restoration to God's Presence in Zion."[11]

God against other gods (40:18–26, 41:21–29, 44:6–20, 46:1–13, 48:1–5, 57:1–13). The theme of highlighting the foolishness of idolatry that was found throughout the first section can also be found in several spots throughout the last section of the book. The common theme is God's power over idols. All the works of God that are clearly seen—both in creation and in the story of Israel—are set in stark contrast to the works made by human hands. Not only do they provide no use, but those who put their trust in idols abandon their *hesed* and reject the LORD.

Water in the Wilderness (41:17–20, 44:1–5, 51:1–3, 55:1–17, 61:11). Isaiah's use of botanical imagery was prevalent in the opening of the book, and spans into the latter half as well. The most common is the picture of God giving water to those who thirst. We have seen in the early chapters how images of wilderness and desert waste are used to show the moral and social decay of the nation of Israel. That image is now reversed as Isaiah looks to a time when God would give life back to His people.

Servant of the LORD (42:1–4, 44:21–22, 49:1–7, 50:4–9, 52:13–53:12, 65:13–16). One of the most popular themes is the collection of Servant Songs found throughout the final chapters of Isaiah. While many immediately think of Jesus when discussing the servant songs, there are some who question the identity of the servant referred to in these verses. A

Biblical Theology of the Book of Leviticus (Downers Grove: IVP Academic, 2015), 205.

11. Morales, *Ascend*, 227.

popular alternative is to see the servant as the nation of Israel. This view is strengthened by the fact that the servant is explicitly identified with Israel multiple times in the book, but the picture doesn't always fit.

> It seems apparent that the servant, though 'Israel' in some sense, is also distinct from exiled Israel ... when viewed in this larger context, the servant is apparently an "ideal" Israel who is closely linked to, but nevertheless distinct from, the sinful nation.[12]

The New Testament writers saw Jesus's death and ministry as a fulfillment of these servant songs and quoted from them often, especially in the gospels. The Ethiopian Eunuch of Acts 8 asks a similar question when reading the servant song, "about whom does the prophet speak?" To which Phillip responds by telling him about Christ.

All Things New (42:5–17, 43:18–25, 54:11–17, 59:14–21, 61:8–9, 62:1–5; 65:17–25). This is somewhat of an umbrella theme, capturing several themes underneath it that all revolve around the idea of God "doing something new." God speaks of a new covenant with His people that is not like the former covenant, but one where sins are wiped away so that both sides may recommit to one another. Similar to the Mountain of the LORD theme is the picture of a new heaven and a new earth where God will rejoice with His people. With images that are picked up in the book of Revelation, Isaiah pictures a removal of all hurt and destruction and a flood of peace and joy.

God's Wrath (42:18–25; 43:22-24; 45:7; 48:9-11; 50:1-3; 51:17-23; 59:1-19; 60:10; 63:1-6; 63:15-65:7; 66:15-24). While many want to separate Isaiah into a book of judgment

---

12. Chisholm, *Handbook*, 100.

(chs. 1–40) and a book of hope (41–66), the line is blurrier than often depicted. While images of hope flood the latter portion of Isaiah, images and warnings of God's wrath are also prevalent. The assurance of union with God is true for those who turn to him (regardless of nationality), but the promise of wrath for those who continually reject God remains. At the close of the book in chapter 66, these two images are juxtaposed as a reminder of these realities.

Future of the Nations (44:24–45:1, 47:1–15, 48:14). The mention of Babylon and Cyrus within the final chapters of Isaiah is one of the main reasons many reject Isaiah's authorship for the entire book. These nations are not mentioned to give a timestamp from different authors, but to continue the theme of God's power over history. In chapter 44, after demonstrating God's power and influence, Isaiah reaches a climax with the naming of Cyrus, "who shall fulfill all my purpose." The emphasis of the chapter is that God is the one who has done and will do these things to and for Israel. It is God who sends Judah into exile, and it will be God who delivers them out of captivity into the security of their own land. While modern critics want to deny any predictive element in the scriptures, it is Isaiah himself "who repeatedly insisted that God alone can tell the future ... and His ability to name the deliverer far in advance is the climactic demonstration of that fact."[13]

Reflection Questions

1. In our section on "What manner of man is the

---

13. Oswalt, *Isaiah*, 512.

prophet," which of the 10 did you see most clearly in Isaiah?

2. Read Rabshakeh's message to Judah in ch. 39 again. What tactics does he use to get them to tempt Israel? How do his tactics mirror the ways we are tempted today?

3. The people are called out for rejecting the hard message of the prophet. They preferred "smooth things" instead. Can we be accused of neglecting the hard parts of scripture and focusing on the "smooth" parts? How does that impact our faith?

4. Trust is a major topic in the historical sections of Isaiah. How can we exhibit trust in God through our daily lives?

5. The "great paradox" of the prophetic message is that Israel will only experience true life after death (exile). How does that message apply to us as New Testament Christians? How do the New Testament writers use death and life to talk about our relationship with Christ?

Chapter 7

The Book of Zephaniah

People do not drift toward holiness. Apart from grace-driven effort, people do not gravitate toward godliness, prayer, obedience to Scripture, faith, and delight in the Lord. We drift toward compromise and call it tolerance; we drift toward disobedience and call it freedom; we drift toward superstition and call it faith. We cherish the indiscipline of lost self-control and call it relaxation; we slouch toward prayerlessness and delude ourselves into thinking we have escaped legalism; we slide toward godlessness and convince ourselves we have been liberated.[1]

— D.A. Carson, *For the Love of God*

AFTER THE LONG and successful reign of Hezekiah, Manasseh would inherit the throne from his father and rule in Judah for 55 years. In that time, he reversed all the good his father had

---

1. D. A. Carson, *For the Love of God*, vol. 2 (Wheaton, IL: Crossway, 1999), Jan. 23rd entry.

done and plunged the nation deep into the waters of idolatry. In 2 Kings 21:1–9 we get a very detailed description of all the sins of Manasseh—the most extensive list of all the kings. Following that description, God sends word that He will officially destroy the nation because of the sin and violence within the city. After his death, his son Amon would take the throne, but only for a short stint. His servants conspired against him and killed the king in his own home. The people of the land then killed the conspirators and placed eight-year-old Josiah on the throne. It is around this time that Zephaniah the prophet comes to deliver his message to the lost, chaotic nation of Judah.

The book of 2 Kings doesn't deviate often when giving a description of Israel's long line of kings, but every now and then, the chronicle breaks to give you a deeper look into the life of a certain ruler. When the story gets to Josiah, we get a detailed look into a key event in the life of this young king. After ordering the Temple to be repaired, a copy of the "Book of the Law" was found by the priest. Upon hearing the contents of this book, Josiah falls to his knees and rends his clothes in remorse. Surely, the LORD is ready to punish the nation because they have rejected the law. Josiah then launches a massive religious reform movement throughout all of Jerusalem, where he stops idol worship, removes pagan altars from the temple, and destroys the high places and other worship sites in the city (extending even into Samaritan territory with the destruction of the temple at Bethel). "Quite significantly, he orders the people to observe the Passover, a much-neglected festival. Without question, Josiah is the greatest reformer the nation ever produced."[2]

2. Paul House and Eric Mitchell, *Old Testament Survey*, 2nd ed. (Nashville: Broadman & Holman, 2007), 169.

* * *

The Political Situation of Zephaniah's Day

After the death of Sennacherib in Assyria, his vengeful brother
Esharaddon took the throne and extended Assyria's influence
into Egypt while also sending and receiving people from
Samaria (Ezra 4:2). His son, Ashurbanipal, would have an even
more powerful reign highlighted by an increased hold on
Egypt, but upon his death, a rivalry for the throne crumbled the
empire. Two of Assurbanipal's sons and a powerful eunuch
fought each other for power, which gave a chance for stability
and peace among vassal nations (such as Judah). "The crum-
bling of Syrian power was felt in Judah ... There are no records
of Assyrian presence in Palestine after 645, and Assyrian
control was certainly gone by 630."[3] This was around the 10th
year of Josiah's reign, which was right before the Book of the
Law was discovered by Hilkiah.

Judah was not the only nation to benefit from the weak-
ening empire. To the south, the Babylonians were slowly
gaining stability and power under their new king Nabopolassar.
Teeming with the Medes and Scythians, Babylon finally
pushed into Assyrian territory around 615 BCE and won the
decisive victory over Nineveh with a siege that lasted only 3
months. A group of survivors fled to Syria in hopes of regaining
strength, but the desperate attempt failed. Babylon would then
take over the Assyrian empire, and the mighty nation would
abruptly come to an end.

* * *

---

3. Arnold and Strawn, *World*, 55.

The book of Zephaniah starts with an odd addition not found in the other prophets. The headings to all the prophetic books often situate the message historically, but that is often the extent of the information they provide. Zephaniah, however, begins his book by tracing his lineage back four generations to a man named Hezekiah. No other information is given, so we can't draw any conclusions for certain, but this move does seem significant. If this is a reference to King Hezekiah, just a few generations ago, it would begin this book with a powerful note of authority. Appealing to Hezekiah would give more information on Zephaniah's status within Judah, but also raise some alarms to the nation that had abandoned all Hezekiah tried to establish.

He takes no time easing into his message as he proclaims that God is planning to sweep away everything from the face of the land. The word "sweep away" primarily means to gather together or collect (such as food for the harvest), but it also has a negative meaning of being destroyed and wiped away (like a strong wind sweeping away everything in its path). Here it is clearly used in the negative. The end of verse 3 makes an even stronger claim, saying, "I will *exterminate* mankind from the face of the earth."[4] In language that many connect to the flood story (Genesis 9:11), God lays out his plan for what sounds like worldwide destruction. "This is an instructive instance in which the language of Prophetic poetry, with its commitment to hyperbole, pushes beyond its intended subject to an incipiently apocalyptic horizon."[5] The whole land, to its very edges, feels the anger of God, and Jerusalem is set up as the target. God is coming to sweep away the idols of the land and all those who are bowed down to them.

---

4. Koehler, et.al, "כרת" *HALOT*, 500.
5. Alter, *Hebrew*, 1341.

"Silence!" declares Zephaniah. This "divine silence" is a call to attention in the presence of one who brings a message from the gods (cf. Judges 3:19; Habakkuk 2:20). He then announces the coming of the Day of the LORD. This day has been announced and alluded to in the prophets already, but receives even greater attention in Zephaniah's message. Other biblical passages also talk about the nearness of this dark and gloomy day where God's anger will be visited upon the wicked, but in Zephaniah, this day is central to his entire message. The Day of the LORD is first pictured as a day of God's sacrifice. All those who are called to the sacrifice are consecrated (lit. "made holy"). Little do these guests know, they are not being purified but being prepared as the sacrifice. Punishment is on the way for those who "array themselves in foreign attire" and "everyone who leaps over the threshold." Both phrases continue the rebuke of pagan worship practices that began at the opening of the book. God is on a search (v. 12), and no one will be hidden from the judgment that is coming. The complacent (lit. "those thickening on the dregs of their wine") will be abruptly awakened from their slumber.

> The metaphor is of aging wine that must rest undisturbed in order to grow richer. The "dregs" or "lees" are the natural sediment that settles to the bottom during this process and must not be shaken up if the wine is to age well. ... Inactivity is good for aging wine. For Yahweh's chosen ... inactivity is complacency.[6]

While the creative portrayal of Judah's complacency is unique to Zephaniah, the sin is not. The prophets have contin-

---

6. James Bruckner, *Jonah, Nahum, Habakkuk, Zephaniah* NIV Application Commentary (Grand Rapids: Zondervan, 2004), 290.

ually sounded the alarm to jar the inhabitants of Jerusalem awake. They implore the people to seek, with all their hearts, the God they once served. "Pursue the God who has protected, nurtured, and blessed you throughout your entire history," they plead. Yet, as Isaiah prophesied, the ears of the people are deaf, their eyes are shut, and their hearts are dull. So, the day of the LORD continues to approach the calloused nation, and Zephaniah reveals the darkness that it will bring. "A day of wrath is that day, a day of distress and anguish, a day of ruin and devastation, a day of darkness and gloom, a day of clouds and thick darkness, a day of trumpet blast and battle cry against the fortified cities" (1:15–16). The nation was warned in the past that their God was a jealous God, and now they see the full force of that jealousy as it consumes and devours the land (1:18).

In chapter 2, they are told to "gather themselves" (the same word used for gathering kindling for a fire) as the day grows nearer and nearer. Yet again, the opportunity is given, "Seek the LORD ... perhaps you may be hidden on the day of the anger of the LORD" (2:3). In repentance there is a chance for protection from the fire that is coming to consume all the wicked cities of the land: the land of the Philistines, the Moabites, the Ammonites, and even to the land of Cush (Egypt). The fire then goes on to consume Assyria, making its way to the capital city of Nineveh and turning the mighty nation into a wasteland. Not only is the city destroyed, but people will walk by her and "hiss and shake their fists" (2:15) as a taunt against the weakened empire. These descriptions of Assyria's destruction will be the same words used in the latter prophets to characterize the downfall and destruction of Judah (cf. Jeremiah 19:8; Lamentations 2:15).

Though they are not the primary target, the second chapter unveils the judgment to come upon the nations surrounding Judah. Some even point out that the nations listed represent the four points on a compass (Assyria to the north, Amon/Moab to the east, Cush (Egypt) to the south, and Philistia to the west) to represent the complete destruction of Judah's enemies. Chapter 3 continues the judgment oracles, but this new city he is speaking of is never named. Verse 1 begins, "Woe to her who is rebellious and defiled, the oppressing city!" But who is he referring to? Before unveiling the identity of the mysterious city, more descriptors are listed. She listens to no voice or correction (3:2), her leaders are ravenous predators (3:3), and her priests profane the law (3:4). Verse 5 contrasts the waywardness of the people with the faithfulness of their God. Although the city is unjust, their God is righteous. Each day He displays His justice within the city, but the inhabitants "know no shame" (3:5). Now the identity of the nation is revealed, not because Judah is named (they are intentionally the only city not called by name), but by the God who is in their midst. This omission is perhaps used to highlight the severity of Judah's corruption. These surrounding nations are full of guilt, but Judah has become so corrupt that Zephaniah can't even bring himself to call them by name.

God hoped that His actions would spur even the smallest trace of repentance, "but all the more they were eager to make all their deeds corrupt" (3:7). In these verses, we find a familiar pattern that is often used in the prophet's message. They begin by calling out the sin of the nation, move to God's attempts to turn the nation back, refuse on behalf of the people, and then a final "therefore" clause where patience and mercy have reached their end, and judgment takes over. Here, the pattern repeats, but with a meaningful difference. Everything is tracking until we reach the "therefore" section (3:8) of Zephaniah's message. "Therefore, wait for me," declares the LORD.

The exhortation to "wait" has a positive connotation here, where it carries the nuance "wait in faith" (see as well Psalm 33:20; Isaiah 8:17, 30:18, 64:4; Habakkuk 2:3). Such hopeful expectation will sustain God's people through the difficult time to come, when God's anger will be poured out on the nations.[7]

All is not dark; there is light at the end of the tunnel. This consuming fire is not meant solely for destruction. In language similar to Isaiah 6, the book shows the purifying effects of the fire. Evil will be consumed, but the remnant will be purified. This remnant is made up of the humble and lowly members of the nation who were hidden by God from the frightful day of wrath. The book ends with a song of jubilation for those who are saved. There is no longer a reason to fear, for the God of Israel is in their midst. The book ends with another gathering of God's people (cf. ch. 1), but this time for good. Those who fear the LORD and humble themselves before Him will be gathered and set as a beacon among the nations.

Tucked into the last two verses is a glimpse of the coming work of Christ. He comes to deal with the sin that has a hold on God's people. He visits the lame and outcasts to give them a place of honor at His table. The gospels often remind us that Christ came first and foremost for the nation of Israel, to gather those who were lost.

> "Behold, at that time I will deal with all your oppressors. And I will save the lame and gather the outcast, and I will change their shame into praise and renown in all the earth. At that time, I will bring you in, at the time when I gathered you together; for I will make you renowned and praised among all

---

the peoples of the earth, when I restore your fortunes before your eyes," says the LORD (3:20).

Reflection Questions

1. Josiah's reforms reach a climax with the observance of the Passover meal. Why is this moment so foundational to his reformation?

2. 2 Kings 23:22 says that the Passover had not been observed since the time of the Judges. Do you think there is a correlation between their negligence in observing the Passover and their spiritual downfall as a nation? How so?

3. If we overlook the importance of the Lord's Supper, how would it influence the spiritual life of the church? How would it influence our personal spiritual life?

4. One of the chief sins for Zephaniah is complacency. How can complacency affect the church?

5. What does it mean for the people of Zephaniah's day to "wait for the LORD"? What does it mean for us today?

6. In our section on "What Manner of Man is the prophet," which of the 10 did you see most clearly in Zephaniah?

Chapter 8

The Book of Nahum

'Aslan is a lion—the Lion, the great Lion.' "Ooh" said Susan. "I'd thought he was a man. Is he—quite safe? I shall feel rather nervous about meeting a lion"... "Safe?" said Mr. Beaver... "Who said anything about safe?" 'Course he isn't safe. But he's good. He's the King, I tell you.' [1]

— C. S. Lewis, *The Lion, the Witch and the Wardrobe*

IF WE TOOK a poll in most churches, Nahum would probably rank as one of the more neglected books of the Bible among Christians. The prophets in general are often overlooked compared to other parts of scripture, but even when we do venture into the prophets, the road typically leads to sections of Isaiah or Jeremiah, not Nahum. There are several possible reasons we could throw out as explanations for the oversight.

---

1. C. S. Lewis, *The Lion, the Witch and the Wardrobe,* in *The Chronicles of Narnia* (New York: Harper Collins, 2001), 146.

The message is brief, spanning only three chapters, and the subject matter is narrow, focused solely on Assyria's destruction. The book is also written in a different style from most of the prophets. Instead of oracles, the book takes the form of a poem. Robert Pfeiffer went so far as to say, "Nahum was not a prophet ... he was a poet."[2] All these factors combined make it tempting to settle for a quick summary of the book, but a deeper dive into the poem yields a powerful message that continues to resonate in our world today.

The book opens with "a *portent* concerning Nineveh."[3] This is not the typical wording for the opening line of the prophets. Based on the other prophets before him, we would expect to see something along the lines of, "and the word of the LORD came to" or "a vision of Nahum." Instead, Nahum begins with *maseh,* which comes from a word meaning "to lift up or to bear" (in this case, it likely has a double meaning: "to lift one's voice" but also "a burden" for Assyria). This is often the term used with judgment oracles against the nations rather than a message from God to His people (cf. Isaiah 13–23, Habakkuk 1:1, Zechariah 9:1). Immediately, we are tipped off that Nahum's message is going to be different than his predecessors. Nahum's task is to lay before the people "the burden of the cup of the curse given to Nineveh to drink."[4] Again, we will see that knowing the history behind the prophets helps unlock meaning within their message.

If you go back in time just a few years prior, Isaiah came to speak to the people of Judah, who were the subjects of Assyrian domination and oppression under Tiglath-Pileser III. Though

---

2. Robert Pfeiffer, *Introduction to the Old Testament* (New York: Harper & Brothers, 1948), 595.

3. Translation from, Alter, *Hebrew*, 1321.

4. Shlomo Yitzchaki, *Commentary on Nahum*, trans. A. J. Rosenberg (sefaria).

the time seemed dark and hopeless, Isaiah assured the people that punishment would not last forever,

> O my people, who dwell in Zion, be not afraid of the Assyrians when they strike with the rod and lift up their staff against you as the Egyptians did. For in a very little while my fury will come to an end, and my anger will be directed to their destruction. And the LORD of hosts will wield against them a whip ... And in that day his burden will depart from your shoulder, and his yoke from your neck (Isaiah 10:24–27).

Isaiah had the courage to stand up during Assyrian oppression and foretell its downfall. Unfortunately for his listeners, that prophecy wouldn't come true until 612 BCE, almost 100 years later. It is Nahum who finally gets to announce that the day Isaiah envisioned has arrived. Nahum has one simple message to give the people: Assyria is coming to an end. This is a welcome message to the nation of Judah, which has lived under Assyria's heavy yoke for some time now. Nahum's "eternal message is one of hope, which gives comfort to anyone oppressed by a long-lasting and seemingly invulnerable tyrant."[5]

Tchaikovsky's 5th Symphony, one of his most popular, begins with a slow, gloomy melody that almost lulls the listener to sleep. At the end of each line, you expect the pace to pick up, but it stubbornly stays on its gloomy course. Three minutes into the composition, a steady beat picks up in the background, almost like the marching of feet in the distance, and the main theme bursts onto the scene, giving a new life to the symphony. One composer compared it to an old war veteran sitting on his

---

5. Aron Pinker, "Nahum: The Prophet and His Message," *JBQ* 33 (2005), 89.

porch recounting the days he was at war. He slowly introduces the setting leading up to the battle, and then the action picks up as the war breaks out around him. Nahum operates in a similar way. It is told from the point of view of someone who witnessed a great and terrifying battle and has escaped to warn all those he can. Nahum begins the message by describing the over-whelming power and vengeance of the God who is at war. In the second chapter, he throws the reader into the chaos of battle, describing the violence of the war at hand. Nahum closes his book by sending a message to the destructive nation, warning them of the doom to come.

The book opens with a tale and description of the God who is coming for the arrogant nation. "A jealous and vengeful God is the LORD. A vengeful God and master of wrath. The LORD takes vengeance on His foes and bears a grudge against His enemies" (1:2). Where the biblical text usually surrounds the Godly trait "slow to anger" with other positive descriptions, here the typical formula is broken and used to describe God's power and justice. All the earth is subject to Him and lies "dev-astated" (v. 5) after encountering His wrath. Who could stand before a God this powerful? Yet, due to His goodness, He also becomes a stronghold for those who take refuge in Him (v.7–8). God then turns to His people and offers a message of hope: the bonds of Assyrian oppression will be broken apart (v. 12–13). Nahum becomes the herald of good news descending from the mountains and delivered to the inhabitants of Jerusalem (v.15).

The second chapter announces the arrival of "the one who scatters" the people. Everyone is frantically called to dress for the battle to come. Following the call comes a vivid description of the terror that wipes through Nineveh (2:3–9). The invaders pour over the walls and rush through the entrance at the gates. They kill, plunder, and tear through the city until all is destroyed. "Desolate! Desolation and ruin!" (2:10) lies the ravaged city. Or as Robert Alter translates more poetically, "Stripped and distraught and despoiled."[6] In Hebrew, the same root is used in all three words to describe the aftermath of war. The core of the word means "to be hollowed out and emptied," but the repetition is used to intensify the destruction. The city is destroyed beyond repair. In somewhat of a mocking taunt, the chapter closes by asking where Assyria, compared to a powerful prowling lion, has now gone. Their city has been wrecked and plundered; nothing remains.

As the third chapter opens, we again encounter the morbid lament seen throughout the prophets, "Woe to the bloody city." This time, it is announcing the death of Assyria. The following verses (2–4) again describe the carnage of the city. The mighty nation that wandered around the Middle East like a lion devouring its prey (2:11) will now stagger like a drunkard through the streets begging for someone to help (3:11). The nation that was once a terror and tyrant over the world will be escorted naked and ashamed before her subjects. Nahum then uses a recent lesson from Assyria's own history to show just how fragile they have become. Thebes, a city in Egypt south of Cairo, was recently taken into captivity by Assurbipal of Assyria. Until that point, no nation had really been able to gain control in Egypt due to its geography and power. The nation that thought they were safe in their land met a devastating loss, and the same is coming for Assyria.

They are told, sarcastically, it seems, to prepare more bricks to fortify their city. Even then, they cannot escape the fate that is coming to devour them.

In a final taunt the prophet compares the stability of Nineveh's leaders to locusts that settle on a hedge on a cold

---

6. Alter, *Hebrew*, 1325.

day, but which depart in every direction when the sun comes out. Assyria's shepherds slumber, her people are scattered with none to gather them (3:18).[7]

In the closing verse, Assyria is again reminded of why destruction is coming: "For upon whom has not come your unceasing evil?" The oppression they wielded will be used against them to their own destruction. In 612 BCE, just a few years following Nahum's ministry, the Assyrian nation was effortlessly overthrown by Babylon, and the first-world power dwindled swiftly to a remnant of refugees in northern Syria. It is at this point that all records of their existence come to an end.

This is the announcement of good news for God's people (1:15): no longer do you have to bear the yoke of Assyrian oppression. The name Nahum means "comfort," which is fitting for the prophet who is endowed with a message of deliverance for his people. It has, however, made people in modern times uncomfortable with the fact that comfort for Israel comes at the price of death and annihilation for others. This problem falls under the umbrella of divine violence in the Old Testament, which appears in several other books. How can a good God condone and even command violence upon others? This element of the Christian religion has come under heavy fire recently, with many different attempts to explain the violence found in scripture. There is a temptation when looking at these texts to explain away or even ignore the harder parts of scripture, but a faithful handling of these difficult passages gives room for both the compassion and justice of God.

From the very beginning, God uses these seemingly polar

---

7. Jack P. Lewis, *The Minor Prophets* (Grand Rapids: Baker Book House, 1966), 58.

attributes to describe Himself to Israel. After being freed in dramatic fashion from Egyptian slavery, the Israelites follow Moses into the wilderness, where they come to learn and know more about the God who saved them. In Exodus 34, God chooses to reveal even more of Himself to Moses on top of the mountain. The description Moses receives presents God as compassionate and patient, but concludes with the reality of His justice. The Lord passed before Moses and proclaimed,

> The LORD, the LORD, a God merciful and gracious, slow to anger, and abounding in steadfast love and faithfulness, keeping steadfast love for thousands, forgiving iniquity and transgression and sin, but who will by no means clear the guilty, visiting the iniquity of the fathers on the children and the children's children to the third and fourth generation (Exodus 34:6–7).

From the very beginning, God wanted His people to know that He is full of grace and compassion, but also of justice. It is important that we remember that balance in a world that is quick to swing the pendulum to one side or the other.

We serve a loving God who does not stand idly by when evil is present among His creation. Terence Fretheim, in his treatment of divine violence, stresses that the violence and anger of God are not divine attributes, but *responses* to human sin and injustice.[8] God's anger and wrath always extend from His care for creation. Heschel explains this element well by comparing it to our care, or lack thereof, for injustice in our world. He claims, "Our sense of injustice is a poor analogy to God's sense of injustice. The exploitation of the poor is to us a

---

8. Terence E. Fretheim, "Theological Reflection on the Wrath of God in the Old Testament," *Horizons in Biblical Theology* 24 (2002): 14–17.

misdemeanor; to God it is a disaster. Our reaction is disapproval; God's reaction is something no language can convey."[9] On the cross, both the wrath and mercy of God are on perfect display. On the cross, the wrath that was meant for us was taken on by one person, God's only Son.

The message of Nahum, while short and narrow in scope, packs a timeless message. While many of us today do not know what life is like at the whim of another nation, we do understand the weight and entrapment of sin in our own lives. Nahum, in a way, foreshadows the message of the gospel. It is the good news coming to those locked in the bonds of oppression, claiming that the evil around us does not have the last word. For Israel, it was Assyria. For us, it is the grip and hold of sin on our hearts. As Paul writes to the church at Ephesus,

> Though you were dead in the trespasses and sins which you once walked, following the course of this world, following the prince of the power of the air ... and were by nature children of wrath, like the rest of mankind. But God, being rich in mercy, because of the great love with which he loved us, even when we were dead in our trespasses, made us alive together with Christ—by grace you have been saved" (Ephesians 2:1–5).

Though the oppressor is different, the same Savior comes to comfort His people.

Reflection Questions

1. What would you say to someone who was

---

9. Heschel, *Prophets*, 284–85.

concerned with the violence they saw in the Old Testament? How can you use that conversation to also highlight the love and mercy of God?

2. In our section on "What manner of man is the prophet," which of the 10 did you see most clearly in Nahum?

3. How would Nahum's message be received by the hearers of his own day? How would an Israelite living under Assyrian oppression respond to what they heard?

4. In what ways does Nahum foreshadow the gospel message?

5. How is the balance of God's love/compassion and His justice displayed on the cross?

6. What other Old Testament passages display a balance of God's justice and mercy?

Chapter 9

The Book of Jeremiah

Perhaps the main task of the minister is to prevent people from suffering for the wrong reasons. Many people suffer because of the false supposition on which they have based their lives. That supposition is that there should be no fear or loneliness, no confusion or doubt. But these sufferings can only be dealt with creatively when they are understood as wounds integral to our human condition. Therefore ministry is a very confrontational service. It does not allow people to live with illusions of immortality and wholeness. It keeps reminding others that they are mortal and broken, but also that with the recognition of this condition, liberation starts.[1]

— Henri J.M. Nouwen, *The Wounded Healer*

IN J.R.R. Tolkien's *Lord of the Rings,* there comes a moment where Frodo soon realizes the gravity of his situation. What he

---

1. Henri J.M. Nouwen, *The Wounded Healer: Ministry in Contemporary Society* (New York: Doubleday, 1972; repr., New York: Image, 2024), 101.

thought would be a joyful and exciting adventure turned out to be the most frightful and challenging trail of his entire life. Weighed down with the burden of the task he must bear, he turns to his confidant and counselor, Gandalf, and says, "I wish the ring had never come to me. I wish none of this had happened." Gandalf sighs and then replies, "So do I, and so do all who live to see such times. But that is not for them to decide. All we have to decide is what to do with the time that is given us." Jeremiah, too, is given an arduous task that consumes and alters his life forever. Yet, both decide to endure the hardship and fulfill the task that has been given to them.

Much like Frodo's journey into Mordor, Jeremiah's life is filled with tears, blood, regret, anguish, and confusion, but also hope and trust. Jeremiah is the last voice the people hear before the holy city of David is destroyed and her people taken into captivity. His voice rings with passion (a word derived from Greek, *pathos*, and Latin, *passio*, to describe intense feeling and suffering) as his prophetic task becomes his greatest burden. Still, he delivers his message to the nation, but the hearts of the people are impenetrable. Beyond the rejection and darkness, he is able to look to a time of hope and salvation for God's people. Jeremiah is one of the hardest of the prophets to read, but in it, we get a window into the life and ministry of God's messengers, unlike any prophet before; a life that closely resembles the work of Christ 600 years later.

Two factors make reading Jeremiah a rather difficult task: chronology and composition. If the constant shift in theme and subject experienced in the earlier prophets seemed burdensome, Jeremiah would only complicate the situation. Not only does Jeremiah bounce abruptly between themes, but he also moves back and forth from poetry to narrative, to history, and even personal prayer. And to put the icing on the cake, none of this is in chronological order. There are several portions that are dated, which is helpful, but there are also large sections that provide only a vague timestamp or none at all (chs. 1–20, 22–23, 30–31, 33, 47–51). Some internal evidence can be used to narrow down a window of time, but most efforts are subjective and offer no definitive solution. Because of these difficulties, we will divide the study between the *Life of Jeremiah* and the *Book of Jeremiah*.

The Life of Jeremiah

> Jeremiah's was a soul in pain, stern with gloom. To his wistful eye the city's walls seemed to reel. The days that were to come would be dreadful. He called, he urged his people to repent—and he failed. He screamed, wept, moaned—and was left with a terror in his soul.[2]

Michelangelo's paintings in the Sistine Chapel feature not only the famous "creation of man" image, but just below it on the side, surrounded by several other figures, is the solemn prophet Jeremiah. Rembrandt would also attempt to bring the suffering of Jeremiah to life through his famous painting of the prophet. He pictures the lonely prophet contemplating in a cave while the city burns in the background. He sits alone, defeated and rejected by those around him. Heschel, Rembrandt, and many others have tried to help us see just how dark a life Jeremiah lived, but maybe there are no words to help us see the pain. There is no art form to make us fully sense the weight he carried. They only give us glimpses, but with those come a deeper appreciation for the rejected minister.

Because of this pain and burden, a unique relationship was

---

2. Heschel, *Prophets*, 133.

born between him and God. The first message sent to the prophet (1:5) has become a hopeful and cheerful verse that is often quoted in celebration of life. For Jeremiah, this call and appointment are just the beginning of his suffering. He will go on to curse the day of his birth and all those who were associated with it. This comes up most powerfully in chapter 20, which contains one of Jeremiah's many "confessions" throughout the book (11:18–12:6, 15:10–21, 17:14–18, 18:18–23, 20:7–13). He begins with a strong claim that God has "seduced" and "raped" him (20:7). "The words used by Jeremiah to describe the impact of God upon his life are identical with the terms for seduction and rape in the legal terminology of the Bible."[3] Like Frodo, he wished this call had never come to him; he wished for his life to be erased from history.

This task, his divine commencement, pushed him to the brink of alienation. Like Rembrandt's portrait, "I did not sit in the company of revelers, nor did I rejoice; I sat alone, because your hand was upon me, for you had filled me with indignation" (15:17). This language of sitting alone used by Jeremiah is the same word used of lepers in Israelite law.

> The leprous person who has the disease shall wear torn clothes and let the hair of his head hang loose, and he shall cover his upper lip and cry out, 'Uncle, unclean.' He shall remain unclean as long as he has the disease. He shall remain unclean. *He shall live alone.* His dwelling shall be outside the camp (Leviticus 13:45–46).

He is commanded by God to refrain from having a family (16:1–13), abstain from weddings or feasting (15:17, 16:8), or

---

3. Heschel, *Prophets*, 144.

funerals (16:5), all of which further isolate him from his own community.

The loneliness and darkness he must face forge his relationship with God. Jeremiah shows us what faith tested by fire looks like. "One of the most important contributions that Jeremiah teaches us about God is the intimate, personal relationship that he reveals. Even during the "dark night of his soul," he struggled with God in an astonishingly open and candid way."[4] In the comments on the prophet Amos, we noted that true worship is taking the heart in whatever state it may be and pouring it before our Creator. This idea is brought to life in the story of Jeremiah. He holds back no emotion when he goes before his God, and in doing so, he teaches us "that we can bring the most intimate of our struggles and concerns before God."[5] How often can we be accused of approaching prayer or worship with a lack of vulnerability? When that happens, our prayers, songs, and petitions become nothing more than a helpline or sophisticated thank-you note. Vulnerability humbles the heart and deepens the relationship we have with our God.

While demonstrating what it means to be vulnerable before God, Jeremiah also shows what it means to faithfully bear the indignation of God (a subject that will be on full display in Lamentations, especially the third chapter). When he first receives his call in the opening chapter, Jeremiah is fearful and timid at the prospect of being God's prophet. He resembles Moses by claiming he doesn't have the skillset or experience to do what God asks and desires that someone else should be chosen. But the prophet is repeatedly sent by God

---

4. William Tuck, "Preaching Jeremiah," *RevExp* 78 (1981), 387.
5. Tuck, "Preaching," 385.

with a new message for the nation, and each time Jeremiah faithfully delivers the message (though sometimes with a fight).

The prophet becomes an example of what Paul speaks of in 2 Timothy 2:15, where he commands Timothy to "rightly handle the word of truth." Throughout that chapter, he encourages Timothy to be mindful of what he teaches but also to remain faithful despite the suffering he may endure or the false teachers around him. Jeremiah must endure both suffering and false prophets during his day as well. While he was prophesying destruction, many would come and deliver a message of peace. Contrary to their selfishness, Jeremiah brings a message that gets him thrown in prison, persecuted, thrown out of the temple, continually rejected, and made a traitor in the eyes of the people. Yet, even with all these obstacles, Jeremiah doesn't hesitate to deliver his message.

Jeremiah compares the word of God to a fire burning in his heart and in his bones (20:7–9). This once timid young aristocrat grows into a prophet who can't help but declare God's word to Judah regardless of the consequences. Jeremiah's dedication urges us to contemplate the influence of the word of God on our own lives. How do we handle the Word of God? What impact does it have on our daily lives? Does it have a deep enough root in our hearts that its fruits can be seen in our daily interactions with others? And most importantly, does it become so important to us that we are willing to abandon everything for the sake of God's word (Matthew 19:28–30)? How we handle the Word of God is crucial (both in doctrine and in practice), and we are called to remain faithful despite any opposition and persecution we might face.

Even with all the harsh treatment he endured at the hands of his countrymen, Jeremiah did not deliver his message with joy. He gained no satisfaction in predicting the coming destruction of his people. "Though he warned that the nation would pass through the refiner's fire, he did so through his own tears."[6] But his tears were mixed with a dash of hope. He, like many of the prophets before him, was also able to look past the fire and know that judgment would not be the last word. In the final days of Zedekiah's reign, when Babylon was besieging the city, Jeremiah went and purchased a plot of land from his relative (32:1–15). This symbolic action showed that "houses and fields and vineyards will again be bought in this land" (32:15). Though encouraging for his nation, Jeremiah would not get to experience this time of renewal. When Jerusalem fell just a year later, Jeremiah was rescued and given special treatment by the Babylonians. He was given the choice to return with them to live in Babylon or to stay with his people and flee in defeat to Egypt. Turning down the lucrative offer, he decides to remain with his countrymen and flee to Egypt, "where he dies in the land of the Pharaohs."[7]

Jeremiah's ministry spanned the reign of five different Judean kings (Josiah, Jehoahaz, Jehoiakim, Jechoniah, and Zedekiah). Each king garnered a vastly different relationship with Jeremiah, presenting him with unique challenges and opportunities with each transition of power. Life under Josiah gave a chance for Jeremiah to experience the prophet's sweeping reforms. It was during this time that Jeremiah received his prophetic call. Had Josiah's reforms really taken root, Jeremiah's life would probably have been much different. Instead, the reforms died with the reformer. After Babylon drove Assyria out of Nineveh in 612 BCE, the remaining Assyrian survivors fled to Syria in a desperate attempt to regain footing.

---

6. Tuck, "Preaching," 385.
7. David Steele, "Jeremiah's Little Book of Comfort," *Theology Today* 42 (1986), 472.

At that time, Egypt began her march to Syria in an attempt to form an alliance with the wounded nation and to prevent Babylon from becoming the new world power. Josiah, seeking an opportunity to gain power, attempted to meet Egypt as they crossed through Judah, hoping to prevent them from joining forces with Assyria. Pharaoh Neco II of Egypt would go on to defeat the attempted blockade, and Josiah was killed in the battle (609 BCE). His son Jehoahaz then takes the throne but only reigns for three months before Neco II comes and takes him as a prisoner and places Eliakim on the throne in his place. Neco II changes his name to Jehoiakim, and Judah officially becomes a vassal state to Egypt. The vassalship doesn't last long, as the vastly important Battle of Carchemish (605 BCE) between Egypt and Babylon leaves King Nebuchadnezzar as the victor and establishes Babylon as the new world power. "From that date Judah's politics was entirely governed by the question of what stance they should take towards Babylon— submission or rebellion."[8]

Life under Jehoiakim would be the most challenging time of Jeremiah's ministry. It was at this time that Jeremiah delivered his famous temple address (Jeremiah 7:26), where "he aroused bitter opposition to himself and his message from all segments of the nation, including his own family."[9] Jeremiah was so at odds with the king that Jehoiakim took the scroll of Jeremiah's prophecy, cut it into pieces, and threw them in the fire (Jeremiah 36). During the fourth year of his reign, Nebuchadnezzar turned from his victory in Carchemish and sought to invade Judah. Though Judah wanted to respond with violence and rebellion, Jeremiah begged the nation to submit to

---

8. Christopher Wright, *The Message of Jeremiah*, Bible Speaks Today Series (Downers Grove: InterVarsity Press, 2014), 21.

9. Charles L. Feinberg, *Jeremiah*, Expositor's Bible Commentary vol. 6 (Grand Rapids: Zondervan, 1982), 359.

the yoke of Babylon. Trying to fight, for Jeremiah, was useless. Only in submitting to the world power would Judah be saved, but her pride would not allow it. Instead, the people saw Jeremiah's message as treason and treated him as the enemy. "Thereafter Jeremiah's life was one of uninterrupted misunderstanding and persecution."[10]

Jehoiakim would eventually lead a rebellion against Babylon, which elicited an immediate response from the powerful nation. Jehoiakim sought an opportunity when Nebuchadnezzar tried to invade Egypt and failed (597 BCE). Jehoiakim dies before having to face the consequences of his actions, and his son Jeconiah would bear the load. After inheriting the throne and rebellion from his father, Jeconiah responds by quickly surrendering the city, which likely saves it from destruction. Nebuchadnezzar would eventually take Jeconiah prisoner (along with other elites, including Ezekiel), place Mattianiah as king, and give him the new name Zedekiah.

Life under Zedekiah was easier for Jeremiah than his predecessors, but Zedekiah proved to be weak and fearful as a leader. Even though he called Jeremiah in for counsel on occasion, he would eventually spurn his advice and go to Egypt for support (589 BCE). Nebuchadnezzar responds by relocating the capital and establishing a non-Davidic ruler as governor. Babylon then laid siege to surrounding cities before reaching Jerusalem in 587 to begin what would become an 18-month siege of the city. Zedekiah attempts to flee in the final moments but is captured. As punishment, he is forced to watch as his sons are executed before him. Immediately after the execution, they gouge his eyes out, making the death of his sons the last thing he sees before being taken as a prisoner into Babylon. Meanwhile, Jeremiah chose to stay with the survivors in

---

10. Feinberg, *Jeremiah*, 360.

Mizpah under the rule of Governor Gedaliah, but he was soon assassinated by a descendant of the house of David (41:1–2), likely out of zeal for the family throne. The remnant community in Mizpah ignored Jeremiah's counsel to surrender and instead fled to Egypt for safety. Jeremiah's ministry would continue with him into Egypt, where his story soon ends, and we hear no more from the tragic prophet.

An interesting question comes up after studying the life of Jeremiah. Is his life and ministry a success or a failure? A complicated question warrants a complicated answer in some cases. If you judge ministry effectiveness by the number of converts, the immediate answer is no. But if we go back to Nouwen's quote above, he describes the work of a minister by saying, "it keeps reminding others that they are mortal and broken, but also that with the recognition of this condition, liberation starts." [11] In this view, the success of Jeremiah's ministry is similar to the ministry of Christ.

There are multiple points in the lives of both these men that parallel one another. [12] Both had a message to deliver to God's nation, but one that also had implications for the entire world. Both were accused of political treason. Both were tried, persecuted, and imprisoned by their own people. Both foretold the destruction of the temple. Even the people during the time of Jesus saw some similarities between the two (Matthew 16:13–14). Both are able to look beyond the current circumstances and tragedy to a time of hope and salvation. More importantly, they both come with a message for God's people, claiming there is a way to true life and communion with God, and both are despised and persecuted for the message they

---

11. Nouwen, *Wounded*, 101.

12. The following parallels and many others can be found in Feinberg, *Jeremiah*, 360–61.

bring. The difference comes in that Jesus fulfills what Jeremiah could only dream of. Jeremiah looked to a day when hearts would be changed. Jesus comes as the one who transforms the hearts of those who follow Him.

The life of Jeremiah is filled with sorrow and pain, yet it also reveals the path of unwavering obedience. One question kept coming to mind while reading through the life of Jeremiah, 'How far am I willing to go in following Christ?' For Jeremiah, there was no end to his obedience. He followed the word of God through persecution, exile, and even death. If I take a realistic look at myself, my commitment to God's path can often end at the first sign of trouble or, at times, temptation. It is important to note that Jeremiah was not perfect. He, too, was a man who was hit by the bulwarks of sin and harassment. We see him struggle with those roadblocks all throughout his life and ministry, but the key is that he does struggle. There are times when we can be accused of making the Christian life seem easy and simple, but it is hardly ever that way. There was nothing easy for Jeremiah. He fought. He wept. He often doubted and questioned what God was doing and longed to quit. Yet, he pressed on even though he could not see the full picture. He trusted God despite the cloud of doubt before him because he knew that judgment was not God's last dealing with His people. He presses on in hope.

> For thus says the LORD: When seventy years are completed for Babylon, I will visit you, and I will fulfill to you my promise and bring you back to this place. For I know the plans I have for you, declares the LORD, plans for welfare and not for evil, to give you a future and a hope. Then you will call upon me and come and pray to me, and I will hear you. You will seek me and find me, when you seek me with all your heart (Jeremiah 29:10–13).

The Book of Jeremiah

In some classical music, operas, and musicals, the work begins with an overture. Each one is different, but the main idea behind an overture is to give a prelude to the show, and they often contain key themes and melodies that appear later on in the story. This is similar to how the book of Jeremiah operates. In the opening chapters of the book, certain themes and images pop up that play a pivotal role later in Jeremiah's message. That is not to say that Jeremiah intended his book to do this, or that it is some literary technique he uses, but it is just simply how the book unfolds. Jeremiah's life and message center around recurring themes that are woven throughout the book. We will look at how those operate in the opening chapters, providing a foundation for understanding them when they reappear.

The book opens by providing the historical context to his life and message. He was born into a priestly family and began his task during Josiah's sweeping reforms. Following Josiah's death, he would have to witness and experience the rapid downfall of his nation into Babylonian captivity. As was already seen in the life of Jeremiah, the shift between these kings has a profound impact not only on the life of the prophet but also on his message to the people. He noticed that although the reforms were successfully implemented in the life of the city, they did not take root in the hearts of the people. They settled for a superficial religion that claimed, "As long as we have the temple and perform the act of worship, God will be with us" (cf. Jeremiah 7–9; 26). Jeremiah tears apart this careless thinking as he proclaims that the nation will be destroyed and the temple lost because of their evil. The heart plays a pivotal role in Jeremiah's message. He mentions it constantly as the source of evil within the nation and as the point of transformation in the new covenant.

Reading through the words of Jeremiah, and especially his complaints to God, you come away with overwhelming evidence that Jeremiah hated his prophetic calling. This is his immediate response upon receiving his call in the opening chapter, and that feeling runs throughout the book (1:4–8, 20:7–8). He despised his mission so much that the day of his conception, when he was "consecrated and appointed," became the worst moment of his life. He longs that this day has never come, yet he continues to proclaim God's message to the people. "In spite of public rejection, in spite of inner misery, he felt unable to discard the divine burden, unable to disengage himself from the divine pathos. He knew why he had to yield; he knew how to explain his inability to resist the terrible errand."[13]

This is the message he is sent to deliver: "See, I have set you this day over nations and over kingdoms, to pluck up and to break down, to destroy and to overthrow, to build and to plant" (1:10). These same words pop up all throughout the book of Jeremiah to describe the scope of God's plan and purpose for Judah and the surrounding nations. From the beginning, God wanted Jeremiah to know that destruction and desolation are not the end of the story. Like the birth pains of a woman in labor, struggle and suffering must be experienced before new life can come forth. These phrases, as Christopher Wright points out,

are drawn from the worlds of agriculture, construction, and warfare, and arranged concentrically in such a way that agriculture begins and ends the list (*to uproot* and *to plant*), construction immediately inside that (*to tear down* and *to*

---

13. Heschel, *Prophets*, 151.

build), while the two warfare metaphors dominate the centre (*to destroy and overthrow*). [14]

Though hope frames the story, the core of the message is destruction, which becomes the major theme of Jeremiah's preaching.

More than any other prophet, God chooses to teach Jeremiah and the people through symbolic actions. This begins with the almond tree and pot of boiling water in the first chapter. The almond tree (Hebrew *"shaqed"*) represents God's "watching over" (Hebrew *"shoqued"*) His word to perform it. There is no changing God's mind at this point. What He says will pass, will pass. For Judah, that entails the certainty of their destruction. This will be done through the wrath of another nation that will spill over (like a boiling pot) from the north and decimate the city. This looks forward to the time when two different kings (Neco of Egypt and Nebuchadnezzar of Babylon) would assert their dominance in the land and eventually surround and take over the city of Jerusalem—a conquest that began in the north and worked its way south to the land of Judah.

These are just the beginning of the many symbolic actions used throughout the book. In chapter 5, Jeremiah searches throughout the city for just one righteous person, illustrating the people's total corruption. In a daunting allusion, God compares the holy city to Sodom and Gomorrah. In chapter 13, Jeremiah is told to wear an old, tattered belt, which represents the fallen relationship of God and Israel. In chapter 18, Jeremiah visits the house of the potter, and there he is shown why God must punish the nation of Judah. In chapter 19, Jeremiah assembles the people in the Valley of Hinnom (cf. Jeremiah 7–

---

14. Wright, *Jeremiah*, 55–6.

8) and smashes a clay jar against the rocks, foretelling the destruction and slaughter of the people. In chapter 25, Jeremiah makes the nations drink from the cup of God's wrath, showing that there is no other choice but destruction. In a political move, Jeremiah takes a wooden yoke and wears it on his shoulders (27:1–28:17), urging the people to submit to Babylonian rule. They instead listen to the false prophet Hananiah, who advises the opposite, and the wooden yoke becomes iron. In an act of hope, Jeremiah buys a field in his hometown of Anathoth (Jeremiah 32), showing that God's people will again be planted in the land. In chapter 35, Jeremiah tests the Rechabites in the temple before the people to show an example of true obedience. Even in Egypt, after the destruction of the city, Jeremiah performs two actions (43:8–13, 51:59–64) to foretell the fate of his people and of Babylon.

God uses these symbolic actions to reinforce His message, but all attempts fail as the people reject His word. It's not that the people fall off or miss the mark every now and then. No, God's bride has forsaken and abandoned her partner. "And I will declare my judgments against them, for all their evil in forsaking me" (1:16—cf. 2:13, 17:13). Multiple allusions are made to the prophet Hosea as Judah is compared to an adulterous woman, a prostitute, and an unfaithful spouse (3:2). He explains, "They have made offerings to other gods and worshiped the works of their own hands" (3:16). Not only is idol worship spoken against, but the activity that comes with idol worship is also exposed. Not only do they build high places of worship, but they stoke a fire and set their children on the altar as a sacrifice (7:30–8:3). Against this, the anger and wrath of God will come.

Jeremiah is sent as "a fortified city, an iron pillar, and bronze walls" (1:18) against Judah. These images of an impregnable city show that Jeremiah will go to war with his own countrymen. They will fight against him and seek to overthrow him, but they will not be able to silence him. This is why God calls him to "gird up his loins" (1:17) for what is to come. It will not be easy, but God reinforces that He is at Jeremiah's side to deliver him (1:19).

> The combination of challenge, command, and promise, is very similar to the commissioning of Joshua, which shows that the prophetic career stretching before him was as daunting as the conquest of Canaan, except that the 'Canaanites' were now his own people.[15]

God, Jeremiah, and the people will struggle and fight with one another until the very end—exile in Babylon and the destruction of Jerusalem (ch. 52).

The opening chapter, like the book as a whole, ends on a small note of hope. "I am with you, declares the LORD, to deliver you" (1:19). God continues to remind Jeremiah that, although there will be pain and heartache, deliverance will come. That is true for Jeremiah, who often finds himself on the brink of death, and it is true for the nation of Israel as well. After recounting the fall of the city and exile in the final chapter, the book ends with an odd story. After a change in power within Babylon, the new king decides to set Jehoiakim free from prison.

> And he spoke kindly to him and gave him a seat above the seats of the kings who were with him in Babylon. So Jehoiakim put off his prison garments. And every day of his life he dined regularly at the king's table, and for this allowance, a regular allowance was given him by the king,

---

15. Wright, *Jeremiah*, 58.

according to his daily needs, until the day of his death, as long as he lived (52:32–34).

This seemingly random story suggests that God is not done with His people and that He will continue to watch over them, even in exile.

Reflection Questions

1. Jeremiah is often called "the weeping prophet." If you were to give him a different title, what would it be and why? (i.e., "the faithful prophet," "the hopeful prophet," "the tortured prophet")

2. Where did Jeremiah get his strength to go on? What gave him the power to move past all the obstacles in his way?

3. Who is someone you have witnessed faithfully cling to Christ in the midst of heartache and pain?

4. What does it mean for me to properly handle the word of God? What does it mean for our churches to faithfully handle the word of God?

5. In what ways was Jeremiah's ministry a failure? In what ways was it a success?

6. What stands out to you the most about the life of Jeremiah?

7. In what other ways does Jeremiah's life resemble that of Christ?

8. What "manner of man" was Jeremiah the prophet?

Chapter 10

The Book of Lamentations

O Lord, the depths of a man's conscience lie exposed before your eyes. Could anything remain hidden in me, even though I did not want to confess it to you? In that case I would only be hiding you from myself, not myself from you. But now my sighs are sufficient evidence that I am displeased with myself ... Whoever I may be, Lord, I lie exposed to your scrutiny. I have already told of the profit I gain when I confess to you. And I do not make my confession with bodily words, bodily speech, but with the words of my soul and the cry of my mind which you hear and understand ... And so I make my confession before you in silence, and yet not in silence. My voice is silent but my heart cries out.[1]

— St. Augustine, *Confessions*

My FORMER TEACHERS might not appreciate this, but I don't

---

1. St. Augustine, *Confessions: Books 9-13*, trans. Carolyn J.B. Hammond (Cambridge: Harvard University Press, 2016), 69–71.

remember much from my 8th-grade trip to Washington, D.C.—
at least, not the educational parts. It was our first big school trip,
filled with memorable experiences, but I wasn't quite mature
enough to fully appreciate everything we saw. Some moments
stand out—the Changing of the Guard, the Eternal Flame,
walking down the beautiful National Mall—but nothing
stopped us in our tracks and made us really reflect on its importance. That all changed the moment we stepped into the Holocaust Memorial Museum. Even a group of middle school boys,
who find it impossible to go five minutes without making a joke
out of something, were easily silenced as we made our way
through each exhibit.

There are several reasons we fill our nation's capital with
memorials and images of those who have fallen. We want to
remember the past, pay homage to those who served their
nation, celebrate victories, and the list could go on. Each memorial prompts a note of respect and sadness, but there is a significant difference when you arrive at the Holocaust Memorial
Museum. Why do we have such a large building dedicated to
such a horrific and hideous event in world history? And what
about this memorial leaves everyone in silence and tears? The
answers are not few. This event in history showed just how
cruel we can be to our fellow man. It displayed the lengths we
would go to obtain power and control. It showed how deeply
hatred corrupts the heart of man. The museum is a profoundly
solemn space, yet it contains a meaningful and redemptive
power. It gives a voice to the voiceless and allows stories to be
told that might otherwise be forgotten. These stories are not
always easy to hear, but it is important that they are
remembered.

The book of Lamentations is brutal, gory, and dark.
Written in the immediate aftermath of Jerusalem's fall in 586
BCE, it vividly recounts the destruction and plunder of the city

in haunting poetry. Its talk of cannibalism, murder, and starvation makes it difficult to read and challenging for modern readers to find meaning amid the devastation. Christopher Wright begins his commentary on Lamentations by addressing those difficulties and tries to show the consequences of its neglect upon the church. He claims that neglecting Lamentations disrespects the voice of those who suffered, deprives the church of "the language of lament," and causes us to forget what it means to wrestle with God. [2]

Just like the halls of the Holocaust Museum, the book of Lamentations "is a *summons to remember* realities endured by real people"[3] during the destruction of God's nation. Without the book of Lamentations, the destruction and fall of Jerusalem would simply be another date in the long line of Judah's history. We have it as part of our Scripture to give voice to those who suffered, but also to remind us of the weight and reality of sin. Over and over again, the prophets emphasize that sin will lead the nation into exile. Yet, the people ignored the voice of God through the prophets. In the final years before captivity comes, Jeremiah pleads with Judah to surrender to Babylon so that they may go in peace and not in bloodshed. Yet, they ignored the voice of God through His messenger. Reading through Lamentations shows us the gravity of Paul's words when he says, "The wages of sin is death" (Romans 6:23).

Lamentations also forces us to be more vulnerable and uncomfortable within our worship. If we are honest, we can probably be accused of making worship into something that is only positive, happy, or upbeat. We want people to walk away from worship uplifted, not sad. Now, this doesn't mean we

---

2. Christopher Wright, *The Message of Lamentations*, Bible Speaks Today Series (Downers Grove: InterVarsity Press, 2015), 19.
3. Wright, *Lamentations*, 19.

should start dressing in all black every other Sunday or look for ways to make the audience cry, but simply a realization that genuine worship can also include some of our uglier emotions. Though rare, this element of worship is not entirely foreign to us. We get glimpses of this during funeral services or moments of prayer in times of tragedy. We see in the Bible numerous stories of people falling to their knees in distress and grief as they bring their burdens before God (cf. Job, Jeremiah, Jesus in the Garden, Paul, and many others). Lament poems are found throughout the Old Testament, giving a voice to the grief endured by God's people.

Each of these gives us an example of what it means to wrestle with God. I remember a conversation I was able to have with a Jewish Rabbi near our home, and after a long talk about some hard topics, he reminded me that wrestling is a key part of his faith. The very name Israel, he said, means "wrestles with God." We may not have all the answers, and the road we are to walk is not meant to be easy, but we are encouraged to keep fighting and know we have a God who is there with us. Lamentations shows faith in action.

The book of Lamentations consists of five separate poems, each containing 22 verses, except for the third chapter, which has 66 verses. The reason for the repetition in number is that each chapter forms an acrostic (each verse begins with the subsequent letter in the Hebrew alphabet, which has 22 letters). There is no obvious reason for the acrostic style. Some say it represents totality, either in the city's destruction or the nation's downfall. Others see more of a theological meaning behind the structure of the poems. David Slavitt sees more of a rhetorical effect, claiming the structure shows "that there is, beyond all the disaster and pain the book recounts, an intricacy and orderly coherence the poetry affirms in a gesture that is encouraging and marvelous."[4] Whatever the writer's intention, it does seem intentional and should not be ignored. The only chapter that is not an acrostic is the final chapter, but it is still written with 22 lines like chapters 1, 2, and 4.

Lamentation 3 Acrostic

The third chapter of Lamentations has more verses than most English Bibles because each individual line is an acrostic, unlike the other chapters, where just the first letter of the stanza is an acrostic. Translations try to point this out by numbering each individual line rather than each stanza. David Slavitt, in his translation, tries to replicate the acrostic style into English to give modern readers a sense of the rhetorical device used by the poet. Here is his translation of the beginning of the third chapter to give a sense of what it is like when read in the original style.

> *Afflicted am I and beset, a man whom God in*
> *his wrath has abased.*
> *Abused by his rod and broken, I am driven into*
> *the darkness.*
> *Against me, he turned his hand, and again and*
> *again.*
>
> *Bones broken, wasted, I am besieged and*
> *battered.*
> *Bitterness is my portion and tribulation.*
> *Banished, I dwell in the darkest darkness like*
> *those long dead.*

---

4. David Slavitt, *The Book of Lamentations: A Meditation and Reflection,* (Baltimore, MD: Johns Hopkins University Press, 2001), xiv.

Chained so I cannot escape and walled in, I am
  a captive.
Crying for help, I call out, but he will not hear
  my prayer.
Crooked are all my paths, which he has blocked
  with boulders.[5]

The poems also switch between different "characters" or "voices" throughout the book. The first poem opens by introducing one of those characters. "How lonely sits the city that was full of people! How like a widow she has become" (1:1). The city of Jerusalem is personified as a lonely widow mourning over her affliction. A common refrain that occurs throughout the book first appears in these opening lines, "she has none to comfort her" (1:2). Lament poems are not uncommon in the Bible. The book of Psalms contains a large portion of lament and mourning, as do most of the prophets. Usually, in psalms or prayers of lament, they are balanced with a message of comfort. Citing several examples, Boda notes that "while the invitation to lament occurs throughout the Prophetic Books (e.g., Jeremiah 9:17–22, Joel 1:8), the summons to joy also is found (e.g., Isaiah 12:6, Zephaniah 3:14–15)."[6] In the book of Lamentations, that balance between comfort and sorrow is wiped out. Six different times, the writer points out that the mourning widow has no one to comfort her. Exile and destruction have been prophesied for many years, but no one listened to the warning. Now the city must actually experience the wrath of their God. Jerusalem must bear the

---

5. Slavitt, *Book*, 73.
6. M.J. Boda, "Lament, Mourning," DOTP (Downers Grove: InterVarsity Press, 2012), 537.

weight of their sins (1:3, 8–9). She sits alone, abandoned, and hopeless, with no one to comfort or protect her.

The city must look on in fear as "she sees other nations enter her sanctuary" (1:10). Jeremiah had already exposed the false assumption that because the temple was in their midst, Jerusalem was protected (Jeremiah 7). He again warns them of this harmful thinking and reminds them that their land and nation were a gift, not a given. If they wanted to remain in the land, they would have to truly repent of their ways, but they ignored Jeremiah and continued to oppress one another. Ezekiel, who prophesies in exile, would see a vision of the presence of God leaving the temple. This signified a withdrawal, not only of God's presence but His protection as well, which allowed Judah's enemies to invade their most holy space. The lonely widow sits helplessly in the streets as chaos ensues around her. The spotlight turns to the widow in verse 12 as she speaks for the first time. Three times she repeats the phrase, "A comforter is far from me" (1:16, 17, 21). With her grief comes confession as the consequences of her sin spill out before her.

The second poem (ch. 2) opens with numerous poetic images of God descending in wrath to consume the nation. The whole city, all the way to the temple (vv. 6–7), melts in the wake of God's presence. All the inhabitants of the city go into mourning (vv. 10–11) as they watch their neighbors die in the streets. In the book of Zephaniah (2:15), Judah and the other nations walked by Nineveh after her destruction, hissing, shaking their heads, and taunting the ruined city. Now those same words are being used for those who pass by Jerusalem. "All who pass along the way clap their hands at you; they hiss and wag their heads at the daughter of Jerusalem: 'Is this the city that was called the perfection of beauty, the joy of all the earth?'" (Lamentations 2:15; cf. Jeremiah 19:8). The city that was meant to be a light to the nations has become a mockery to all those who pass by. The closing verses of chapter 2 paint the harsh reality of the destruction and chaos that flood through the city.

Chapter 3 is probably the most well-known part of Lamentations, and for good reason. It gives a beautiful portrait of faith amid darkness as the poet's tears are quelled with hope. But who is the poet? His voice has appeared, but he never identifies himself. Tradition has ascribed the book to Jeremiah largely due to the Septuagint and 2 Chronicles 35:25. The Septuagint (a Greek translation of the Old Testament that began in 250 BCE and was completed in the years following) begins the book by saying, "And it came to pass after Israel had gone into captivity, and Jerusalem was laid waste, that Jeremiah sat weeping and composed this lament over Jerusalem." The verse in 2 Chronicles 35 states that Jeremiah had composed laments for the death of King Josiah. While it is hard to know for certain, the arguments against Jeremiah's authorship seem forced. Chapter 3 gives a picture of a man who has endured great affliction, both from God and his own people, yet still looks to his God for salvation. Powerful connections can be made to Jeremiah, but still, the writer chooses to remain anonymous. It is important to remember that he speaks for the nation, not for himself.

The famous plea in the middle of the book (3:21–30) isn't used to highlight his great faith but to model the mindset he wants his own people to adopt. While he speaks in the first person, he does so with the community in mind. All of Jerusalem has been "besieged and enveloped with darkness and tribulation" (3:5). Through all the pain, the poet urges the people to remember their God. Though His anger has come, that will not be the end. He urges the people to wait. Bear the punishment of the LORD for just a while, then we will experience His compassion and comfort. But waiting should not be idle. "Let us test and examine our ways and return to the LORD!" (3:40). While we wait, we are to examine ourselves, turn to the LORD, and confess. Confession becomes the first step on the road to repentance. The word "test" means to pick through carefully and find what is good and what needs to be thrown out. [7] This is where the book finds its strongest connection with our modern world. Just as it was needed for God's people then, this cycle of examination, confession, and repentance should be an ongoing rhythm in the lives of God's people today.

Chapter four continues the poetic depiction of the horror that has taken over the city. The temple is torn down and scattered, the people have been beaten down, and the young die of hunger and thirst in the streets of the city. All the pain is because "the iniquity of the daughter of my people has been greater than the sin of Sodom" (4:6). Prophets in the past have compared Jerusalem to the sinful cities from Genesis before, but this time Jerusalem is said to have surpassed their iniquity. Though they were once the prized and pure possession of God, they have ruined their garments and become so unclean that they are now untouchable outcasts (4:7–8, 13–15). The city lies bare, exposed, and helpless (4:17).

The final chapter is the only chapter in the book that is not an acrostic. There are several reasons that have been proposed, but no perfect answer. Perhaps it is a purposeful counter to the order found in the book's beginning. If Slavitt's comments about the hope and encouragement provided by the structure are true, the lack of that order toward the end is very telling. It's as if everything that once made sense to the poet is now gone. The small bit of hope he had in salvation is fleeting. All that is

---

7. Koehler, et.al, "חפש" *HALOT*, 341. see also, Genesis 31:35; Proverbs 2:4; 20:27.

left is chaos. The chapter is a prayerful plea for God to take a true look at the situation of His nation and people. The poet speaks of the hardships they are having to bear and then finishes with a powerful question. Why is this happening? Why has God turned His back on the nation He loves? These questions are left in the air with no answer and provide a perfect transition to Habakkuk, the final pre-exilic prophet.

Reflection Questions

1. If Jeremiah is the poet, what major differences do you see between this short book and the longer Book of Jeremiah? What similarities did you recognize?
2. What role/purpose do you think the acrostic form of Lamentations serves? How does it influence the meaning of the book?
3. What does the phrase "wrestle with God" mean to you? How do we make that a part of our faith?
4. What does it mean to really examine your life? When you do examine your life, what do you find? How can we make self-reflection/examination a habit in our lives?
5. Do we neglect the practice of confession in the church today? How can we make confession a larger part of our daily walk?
6. How do you think the people of Judah would have received Jeremiah's lamentation? Would it have provoked a response or been ignored? Why?

Chapter 11

The Book of Habakkuk

I am a child of this age, a child of unfaith and doubt, up to this day and even ... to the coffin lid ... And yet, God gives me sometimes moments of perfect peace; at such moments I feel that I love and believe, that I am loved by others; and during such moments I formulated a creed of my own wherein all is clear and holy to me. This creed is as simple as this: I believe that there is nothing and no one more beautiful, deeper, more sympathetic and more reasonable, courageous and more perfect than Christ.[1]

— Fyodor Dostoevsky, *Letters of Fyodor Michailovich Dostoevsky to His Family and Friends*

HABAKKUK IS unlike the other prophets of his time. He is a

---

1. Fyodor Dostoevsky, *Letters of Fyodor Michailovich Dostoevsky to His Family and Friends*, trans. Ethel Colburn Mayne (London: Chatto & Windus, 1917), 67.

protester who brings the cries of the people before God and demands an answer. We saw in Jeremiah an example of vulnerability before God. In Lamentations, we saw a realization of the corruption within the city and what it means to bear the anger and wrath of God. Habakkuk, in the style of Job, shows us what it means to protest God. Interestingly, though, neither Habakkuk nor Job is given an answer to their questions. At least, not the answer they, or the reader, would expect. Instead, they are given a display of God's power that guides them along the path to understanding. This marks the difference between their complaint and protest and, at times, our own. Both these men walk away from their meeting without a single answer to any of their questions—and they are seemingly okay with that response. They approach God with questions and come away with a deeper knowledge of God, which leads to hope.

The book of Habakkuk takes the form of a dialogue between the prophet and God. In all other prophetic books (except for perhaps Jonah), the prophet comes with a message from God to the people. Habakkuk reverses the role as he comes before God with a heavy slate of questions on behalf of the people. Where the earlier prophets came with accusations against the people, Habakkuk came with accusations against God. Where the former prophet pleads for the people to repent, Habakkuk begs God to wake up and act.

Very little is known about the prophet Habakkuk, leaving several questions about the composition of the book. Most ambiguous of all is the date of his prophecy. There are some elements that assume the Babylonian reign has already taken place, while other passages imply that the Babylonian rise has yet to happen. Following the thought of Chisholm, "Perhaps the best way to resolve the problem is to understand the book as a collection of messages from different periods in the prophet's career."[2] Although the date is difficult to determine, ending with this book provides a perfect transition into the post-exilic prophets, who must heed God's advice to Habakkuk and wait for the coming day of God's salvation.

Habakkuk opens with his primary complaint against God. "How long," he cries out, "will you not hear and not save?" He complains to a God he sees as inactive and idle. Why does God sit by while evil wins the day and "the law goes forth paralyzed" (1:4)? The word "paralyzed" is used elsewhere in the Bible for the heart or hand going numb. Jacob's heart, when he first hears news that Joseph is still alive in Egypt, is said to have "gone cold (or numb)" because he did not believe the report. This same word is used to describe the effects of God's law within His own nation. It has been abandoned, violated, and ignored, "causing the law to be incapacitated, as it were."[3] Habakkuk asks God to look at all the violence taking place in his city, "How long will you let this go on without punishment?"

God responds in verse 5, but not in the way Habakkuk would have anticipated. "Look around," God commands him, "for I am doing a work in your days that you would not believe if told" (1:5). This shouldn't have been much of a surprise to the prophet. How often has God operated within the limits of what humans thought possible or expected? But that is not the end of God's reply. He goes on to tell Habakkuk exactly what His plan is, and it is not the answer the prophet wants. The Chaldeans (another term for the Babylonians throughout the Old Testament) will be the agent through which God's judgment will come upon the wayward inhabitants of Jerusalem.

Habakkuk again protests God's plan. "This doesn't make

---

2. Chisholm, *Handbook*, 433.
3. Chisholm, *Handbook*, 435.

sense," the prophet replies. How can you use an even more wicked and sinful nation against your own people? We are not great, but we are at least more righteous than the Babylonians. If they are allowed to continue their destruction, there will be no stopping their empire (1:17). The LORD responds by telling Habakkuk that judgment will also fall upon Babylon for all their evil. Though they are used as an instrument for God's judgment, they too must face that judgment in due time. "The man whose soul is not upright within him shall fall. Wickedness will destroy itself. It will burst as a bubble; it will collapse as a wall; but the righteous man will live by his faithfulness."[4] Chapter 2 closes with a long list of woes against the Babylonian nation. They are accused of five key sins that will lead to their downfall: they steal and plunder, dishonest personal gain, violence and oppression of others, corrupt leadership, and idolatry. Each of these sins is addressed in detail as God assures Habakkuk that they will not walk away unscathed.

Tucked in the opening of the second chapter is one of the most well-known passages in the book of Habakkuk. The second half of verse 4 reads, "But the righteous man lives through his faithfulness."[5] Three different times this verse is quoted in the New Testament (Romans 1:17, Galatians 3:11, Hebrews 10:38), which warrants a detour to look at it in more detail. When studying this passage (or any Old Testament scripture that is quoted in the New Testament), it is important to first understand what the passage means in its original context. Only then can we see how the New Testament writers use it in their context and message, allowing us to make stronger applications in our own lives.

After protesting God's plan to use Babylon as a means of

---

4. Lewis, *Minor*, 64.
5. Translation by Alter, *Hebrew*, 1334.

executing justice for Judah, Habakkuk is given a vision and told to write it on a scroll. Unlike most visions in the prophets, "Habakkuk's vision remains unknown to us. Its content is not put into words ... There is an answer to Habakkuk's question. It is an answer, not in terms of thought, but in terms of events."[6] God *will* act *for* the salvation of His people. The day of Israel's redemption *will* come. "If it tarries, wait for it" (Habakkuk 2:3). They must wait in hopeful expectation for the vision's fulfillment. "True, the interim is hard to bear; the righteous one is horrified by what he sees. To this, the great answer is given: "The righteous shall live by his faith" ... Prophetic faith is trust in Him, in whose presence stillness is a form of understanding."[7] This same faithfulness in the presence of darkness is what Paul seeks from his audience when writing Romans and Galatians. This hope and eager expectation for Christ is what the writer of Hebrews stresses at the end of chapter 10 (as opposed to those who "shrink back" in their faith). In both the Old and New Testaments, waiting becomes the essence of faith —we eagerly anticipate Christ's return.

The final chapter takes the form of a prayer to God. Habakkuk recalls God's mighty works throughout history and begs God to revive His action in the present (3:2). He prays that God would act again, but also that "in wrath, He remembers mercy." Habakkuk's prayer unfolds before his eyes as he sees God descend in majestic power to destroy the enemy. The nations that oppressed others and committed evil were wiped out all for the sake of His own. "You went out for the salvation of your people, for the salvation of your anointed. You crushed the head of the house of the wicked" (3:13). The powerful vision leaves the prophet trembling in fear. He responds in the

---

6. Heschel, *Prophets*, 182.
7. Heschel, *Prophets*, 182.

only way he knows how—silence. "Yet I will quietly wait for the day of trouble to come upon people who invade us" (3:16).

The book ends with a beautiful prayer and a powerful declaration of faith.

> Though the fig tree should not blossom, nor fruit be on the vines, the produce of the olive fail and the fields yield no food, the flock be cut off from the fold and there be no herd in the stalls, yet I will rejoice in the LORD; I will take joy in the God of my salvation. GOD, the Lord, is my strength; he makes my feet like the deer's; he makes me tread on my high places" (Habakkuk 3:17–19).

Habakkuk is a man who is so heavily burdened by all the evil and corruption around him that it drives him before God in protest, asking the difficult question, "Why?" God answers, but "the response given to him is not the comfort of explanation."[8] Instead of an explanation, he is given an encounter—one that reshapes his understanding and challenges him to trust. Much like the story of Job, instead of seeing God's plan, he sees God's power. Habakkuk's many questions fade in the presence of the LORD as the vision he receives drives him to hope.

One of the more abstract elements in the book of Habakkuk is the way it handles the problem of evil. Even though the book remains silent, many writers and thinkers throughout history have tried to supply an answer to the difficult questions raised by Habakkuk. The problem of evil and suffering has been the subject of numerous debates throughout history, as each era offers new ways to deal with the issue. It is interesting, however, that the biblical authors never try to give an answer to the problem. Job and Habakkuk both raise the questions, but come

---

8. Heschel, *Prophets*, 179.

away with no explanation, and neither of them seems eager to fill the void. Instead of providing answers in these difficult moments, God chooses to go a different route.

John Lennox, a renowned apologist from Oxford, was asked to speak on the problem of evil and suffering to a group of students at Stanford University. Many gathered to hear his take on the issue, but he provided an answer they likely didn't expect. His answer was simply, "We don't know." We don't know exactly why evil and suffering exist in the world, but there is something we do know. Lennox then points his audience toward the cross. The heart of Christianity, he claims, is the cross, but what is God doing *on* the cross? He concludes that it is because "God does not become distant with the problem of human suffering but has Himself become part of it."[9]

Instead of answers, God wants us to remember His presence. This shows up throughout Israel's history. The wilderness wanderings show God unmistakably in Israel's midst by day and by night. The temple signified God's presence within the city. The stories of Daniel and Esther make this a key part of their message, showing how God is with His people even in exile. The very name of Jesus, Immanuel, is a reminder that God has not forgotten His people. The gospel of John echoes that thought by saying that Christ came to dwell (literally, "tabernacle") among His people. Then there is the cross where God chooses to become present with His people in a profoundly new way. There, in a moment of deep suffering and darkness, our God chooses to dive into the depths of evil and death to provide us with an escape. And this same God assures

---

9. John Lennox, "The Loud Absence: Where is God Amidst Suffering and Evil?" *The Veritas Forum* speech at Stanford University. https://youtu.be/huw4cg_PYIA?si=7NRtCgoePaBDJoQP.

us with these comforting words before ascending to heaven, "Surely I am with you always, to the very end of the age" (Matthew 28:20).

Reflection Questions

1. How can we make vulnerability, protest, and lament a bigger part of our worship (personal and congregational)?

2. Do you believe that even today God is "doing a work that you wouldn't believe if told?" If so, how does that change your outlook on the world? How does that influence your mission in life?

3. In Habakkuk's prayer of faith (3:17–19), he takes moments from everyday life to describe his faithfulness (fruit of the vine, food in the field, livestock in the pasture ...). Even without these fundamental parts of his life, he will still be faithful. If you were to fill in Habakkuk's prayer with moments from your own life, what would you add? (Though there be no ... gas in the car, food in the pantry, check at the end of the week, etc.). Write your own prayer of faith.

4. In what ways have you encountered the question of evil and suffering in the world? What helped you through those challenging times?

5. What are some other instances in scripture that focus on God's presence with His people? How is God present with us today?

Works Cited and Further Reading

Alter, Robert. *The Hebrew Bible: A Translation with Commentary*. 3 vols. New York: W. W. Norton, 2019.

Arnold, Bill and Brent Strawn, eds. *The World Around the Old Testament: The People and Places of the Ancient Near East*. Grand Rapids: Baker Academic, 2016.

Augustine. *Confessions: Books 9–13*. Translated by Carolyn J.B. Hammond. Cambridge: Harvard University Press, 2016.

Barnes, Julian. *A History of the World in 10 ½ Chapters*. New York: Random House, 1990.

Beale, G. K. and D. A. Carson, eds. *Commentary on the New Testament Use of the Old Testament*. Grand Rapids: Baker Academic, 2007.

Bickel, Bruce and Stan Jantz. *What Ticks God Off: The Ways We Irritate God and What We Can Do About It*. Nashville: Thomas Nelson, 2001.

Boda, Mark J. and J. Gordon McConville, eds. *Dictionary of the Old Testament Prophets*. Downers Grove: IVP Academic, 2012.

Bright, John. *A History of Israel*. 3rd ed. Philadelphia: Westminster Press, 1981.

Bruckner, James. *Jonah, Nahum, Habakkuk, and Zephaniah*. NIVAC. Grand Rapids: Zondervan, 2004.

Brueggemann, Walter. "What Naboth Teaches Us Today: Part II." https://churchanew.org/brueggemann/what-naboth-teaches-us-today-part-ii

Bunyan, John. *The Poetry of John Bunyan*. Portable Poetry, 2017.

Carson, D.A. *For the Love of God*. Vol. 2. Weaton, IL: Crossway, 1999.

Chan, Michael J., and Brent A Strawn, eds. *What Kind of God? Collected Essays of Terence E. Fretheim*. Winona Lake: Eisenbrauns, 2015.

Chisholm Jr., Robert B. *Handbook on the Prophets*. Grand Rapids: Baker Academic, 2002.

Dearman, Andrew J. *The Book of Hosea*. NICOT. Grand Rapids: Eerdmans, 2010.

Dostoevsky, Fyodor. *Letters of Fyodor Michailocitch Dostoevsky to His Family and Friends*. Translated by Ethel Colburn Mayne. London: Chatto & Windus, 1917.

Erickson, Amy. *Jonah: A Commentary*. Grand Rapids: Eerdmans, 2021.

Feinberg, Charles. *Jeremiah*. EBC 6. Grand Rapids: Zondervan, 1986.

Fretheim, Terence E. "God and Violence in the Old Testament." *Word and World* 24 (2004): 18–28.

———. "Theological Reflections on the Wrath of God in the Old Testament." *Horizons in Biblical Theology* 24 (2002): 1–26.

———. *Reading Hosea-Micah: A Literary and Theological Commentary.* Macon, GA: Smyth & Helwys Publishers, 2013.

Garrett, Duane A. *Hosea and Joel.* The New American Commentary. Nashville: B&H Academic, 1997.

Gentry, Peter J. *How to Read and Understand the Biblical Prophets.* Wheaton: Crossway, 2017.

Grogan, Geoffrey W. *Isaiah.* EBC 6. Grand Rapids: Zondervan, 1986.

Heschel, Abraham. *The Prophets.* New York: Harper Collins, 2001. Kindle edition.

House, Paul and Eric Mitchell. *Old Testament Survey.* 2nd ed. Nashville: Broadman & Holman, 2007.

Kaiser Jr., Walter. *Hard Sayings of the Bible.* Downers Grove: InterVarsity Press, 1996.

Koehler, Ludwig and Walter Baumgartner. *The Hebrew and Aramaic Lexicon of the Old Testament.* Leiden: Brill, 2000.

Lennox, John. "The Loud Absence: Where is God Amidst Suffering and Evil?" *The Veritas Forum* speech at Stanford University, 2011. https://youtu.be/huw4cg_PYIA?si=7NRtCgoePaBDJoQP.

Lewis, C. S. *The World's Last Night and Other Essays.* New York: Harper Collins, 1952.

———. *The C.S. Lewis Signature Classics.* New York: Harper Collins, 2017.

———. *The Chronicles of Narnia.*

Lewis, Jack P. *The Minor Prophets.* Grand Rapids: Baker Book House, 1966.

Lim, Bo and Daniel Castelo. *Hosea.* Two Horizons Old Testament Commentary. Grand Rapids: Eerdmans, 2015.

Miller, Maxwell J. And John H. Hayes. *A History of Ancient Israel and Judah.* 2nd ed. Louisville, KY: Westminster John Knox Press, 2006.

Morales, Michael L. *Who Shall Ascend the Mountain of the Lord?: A Biblical Theology of the Book of Leviticus.* Downers Grove: InterVarsity Press, 2015.

Motyer, Alec J. *The Prophecy of Isaiah: An Introduction and Commentary.* Downers Grove: InterVarsity Press, 1993.

Nouwen, Henri J. M. *The Wounded Healer: Ministry in Contemporary Society.* New York: Doubleday, 1972. Reprint New York: Image, 2024.

Oswalt, John N. *Isaiah.* NIV Application Commentary. Grand Rapids: Zondervan, 2003.

Pfeiffer Robert. *Introduction to the Old Testament.* New York: Harper & Brothers, 1948.

Pinker, Aron. "Nahum the Prophet and His Message." *JBQ* 33 (2005): 81–90.

Shackelford, Don. *Isaiah*. Truth For Today Commentary. Searcy, AR: Resource Publications, 2005.

Slavitt, David R. *The Book of Lamentations: A Meditation and Translation*. Baltimore, MD: Johns Hopkins University Press, 2001.

Smith, Gary. *Hosea, Amos, and Micah*. NIV Application Commentary. Grand Rapids: Zondervan, 2001.

Steele, David. "Jeremiah's Little Book of Comfort." *Theology Today* 42 (1986): 471–477.

Tolkien, J.R.R. *The Lord of the Rings: Return of the King*. Boston: Houghlin and Mifflin, 1955.

Tozer, A.W. *The Pursuit of God*. Harrisburg, PA: Christian Publications, 1948.

Tuck, William. "Preaching from Jeremiah." *RevExp* 78 (1981): 381–395.

van der Walt, Chris. "Peace is not the Absence of War but the Presence of a Relationship Founded by God—שלום (*shalom*) in Isaiah and Micah." *In die Skrifling* 55 (2021): 1–8.

Waltke, Bruce K. *An Old Testament Theology: An Exegetical, Canonical, and Thematic Approach*. Grand Rapids: Zondervan, 2007.

Wiesenthal, Simon. *The Sunflower: On the Possibilities and Limits of Forgiveness*. Rev. ed. New York: Schocken Books, 1998.

Wolff, Hans Walter. *Micah the Prophet*. Translated by Ralph D. Gehrke. Philadelphia: Fortress Press, 1978.

Wood, Leon J. *A Survey of Israel's History*. Rev. ed. Grand Rapids: Zondervan, 1986.

Wright, Christopher J. H. *The Message of Jeremiah*. Bible Speaks Today Series. Downers Grove: InterVarsity Press, 2014.

———. *The Message of Lamentations*. Bible Speaks Today Series. Downers Grove: InterVarsity Press, 2015.

Also by Cypress Publications

The Christian Life: Chapters for Bible Teachers
by Ed Gallegher

Ecclesiastes: A Document Designed to Disturb
by Coy Roper

Equipping the Saints: A Practical Study of Ephesians 4:11–16
by Bill Bagents and Cory Collins

Jesus the Christ: Chapters for Bible Teachers
by Ed Gallagher

Silly Songs, Surprising Stories, and Supreme Court Justices: The Wild Fun-tier of Stone-Campbell Movement History
by John Young

Supporting Sisters: A Biblical Approach to Helping One Another Through Life's Struggles
by Kim Chalmers

WHAM! Facing Life's Heavy Hits: Thirteen New Testament Encounters
by Bill Bagents and Laura S. Bagents

WHAM! Facing Life's Heavy Hits: Thirteen Old Testament Encounters
by Bill Bagents and Laura S. Bagents

CYPRESS
PUBLICATIONS
An Imprint of Heritage Christian University Press

To see a full catalog of Heritage Christian University Press and its imprint Cypress Publications, visit
www.hcu.edu/publications